4.00

SOVIET PASSAGE

JON HUMBOLDT GATES

edited by
BEVERLY HANLY

Best Wishes,
Jon Humboldt Gates

Summer Run
PUBLISHING

Books by the author

Falk's Claim
Night Crossings
Soviet Passage

Yuri and *It's Warm in Siberia* first appeared in
Northcoast View Magazine

Photos on pages 59 and 136 first appeared in
Fine Homebuilding Magazine

Grateful acknowledgement is made to reprint excerpt from
Almost at the End, by Yevgeny Yevtushenko, on page one; and
Yevtushenko interview in *The Progressive*, April, 1987,
on page 116.

PUBLISHED BY:
SUMMER RUN PUBLISHING
1111 B STREET
EUREKA, CALIFORNIA 95501

PRINTED IN THE UNITED STATES
ISBN 0-923000-00-3

Foreword

This trip began long before the 747 lifted off the runway in San Francisco, bound for Tokyo and a ship to the U.S.S.R. It might have begun under my school desk in the late 1950's, practicing bomb drills. Or maybe it began the night a thunderous bolt of lightning struck the Catholic church, a few hundred feet from our home. After the big crack, the house shook as though an earthquake had hit. My father sat straight up in bed and said the Russians had dropped an atomic bomb. I was six years old, and petrified.

I grew up thinking that Russians hated Americans. I was one of the millions of American kids who watched civil defense test patterns on TV. Nikita Khrushchev pounded his shoe on the table at the U.N., and the Cuban missile crisis mushroomed. Soviet armored divisions paraded with atomic rockets on Red Square. America dug bomb shelters.

As kids, we learned to talk about what we wanted to be when we grew up, despite the awareness that our future was wired for global destruction.

The Soviet ship, *Khabarovsk*, was a miniature U.S.S.R., sailing across the sea of Japan toward Siberia, broadcasting Russian music and announcements over the ship's address systems and serving Russian food. Years of buried fear made the crew seem more exotic than average human beings. Cyrillic signs marked the passageways. Red and gold Soviet flags snapped in the breeze.

I stood at the bow of the *Khabarovsk* and watched for the coast of Siberia. We hadn't seen land in two days. An older man from Hiroshima leaned against the rail alongside me, talking about life in his city after the war. We listened to the hiss of white water and the cry of seagulls as gray ocean mists gave way to a long dark rampart across the horizon. My first glimpse of Russia.

Only a week before, I'd been with my father aboard his commercial fishing boat off the coast of northern California, a small American flag hoisted in the sunlight. I had lived most of my life in the redwood forest region, around the small seaport of Humboldt Bay, an area balanced delicately between wilderness and industry. Russian fur traders charted the bay almost two centuries ago. I read their travel journals while writing local folk stories.

What began as a simple curiosity over a few Russian diaries, turned into a full-blown obsession. A stack of books ranging from Tzar wars to Soviet science fiction and two years of Russian language study culminated in a trip to the U.S.S.R..

Redwoods to Red Square was a big jump. I wanted to enter Russia slowly, and ride the Trans Siberian Express across the countryside. I could have flown over the Atlantic and landed in Moscow, but I'd heard that Muscovites were just as impatient and hurried as New Yorkers, and I'd never found New York City an easy place to meet people.

I wondered how Russians would react to an American traveling alone, since nearly all foreigners visited the U.S.S.R. in groups or with guides. My entire trip had been arranged through the Soviet travel bureau. Individual travel was more expensive, but being herded around to official exhibits didn't appeal to me. I wanted to drive on country roads, see the backstreets, and eat in public diners.

The Soviet Union defied comprehension. Spanning eleven time zones, the U.S.S.R.'s fifteen republics contained more than one hundred languages and a variety of lifestyles based on European, Middle Eastern, and Asiatic cultures. Millions of people in the outlying republics didn't speak the Russian language. Traveling for two months in Russia would not unravel any Soviet political mysteries. I would only glimpse a few aspects of a deeply layered Soviet society.

That last afternoon at sea, I watched the approaching dark coastline of Eastern Siberia slowly develop into rocky bluffs and hills of green grass. An ivory lighthouse rose near the entrance to Nakhodka Harbor.

Two sailors stood near the anchor winch. Their Russian conversation faded in and out beneath the deep rumble of ship's engines and the sound of the bow wash as the Kabharovsk broke through the waves.

I was riding the crest of a twenty-five-year wave of fear and fantasy. All the dreams and nightmares I'd had about Russia were behind me. By sunset, I would be aboard the Trans Siberian Express.

"... I suppose
    that at first, it was people who invented borders,
and then borders
        started to invent people." —Yevgeny Yevtushenko—

Shimonovsk Station

B*abushka*!" A station porter shouted as an elderly woman stumbled back over his luggage cart. He sprang quickly and caught the frightened woman before she hit the wet concrete platform. She had been waving to someone on the train. The porter held her until she could steady herself. Graciously, the old grandmother straightened her coat and thanked him.

I stood in line at a small food kiosk, entranced by the sounds and smells of a rainy morning at Shimonovsk Station, near the Chinese-Soviet border. Across the rail yard, near a pile of concrete ties, a dozen workers stood around a bonfire. Some of the crew wore heavy quilted jackets with their pants tucked into tall black leather boots.

Rain sprinkled lightly across my face and made puddles on the cement platforms. The smell of hot steel brakes and rail bed creosote mingled with drifting bonfire smoke and burning coal. I had never wondered how the air might smell in a Siberian rail town during a summer rainfall.

When I awoke that morning, the landscape of Siberia looked familiar, like the inland mountains and valleys of the Pacific Northwest. The seven-foot-square, second-class cabin seemed stuffy. Then I remembered. I wasn't on Amtrak. I looked at the other bunks where an old man and the young Soviet soldier I'd talked to the night before were still asleep. I was in Russia.

The kiosk line moved slowly. My mind raced as my turn came, trying to figure out what I wanted to buy and to remember the Russian word for it. I felt nervous speaking Russian in such a hurried situation. Unfamiliar words and slang expressions flew past my ears unrecognized. All my classroom confidence vanished.

Pomidor, pomidor, pomidor, I said to myself, practicing the word for tomato. At the kiosk window, an old woman in a long flowered dress moved quickly, taking people's orders and lining up the items on the worn wooden counter. The man in front of me filled a netted bag with food.

Since leaving the eastern seaport of Nakhodka two days before, Trans Siberia had stopped at many towns along the tracks, sometimes for only five minutes. I glanced at the train to make sure it wasn't creeping out of the station.

I didn't want to be left in Shimonovsk without a passport or luggage. My cabin was near the end of the train, a long way from the station kiosks.

The conductors stood waiting along the platform with their yellow signal flags in hand. They eyed their watches. The mechanics were out from under the train. I was about ready to run for my car.

"Da, shto toy xocheesh?" Yes, what do you want? The old woman listened blindly for my order. I thought I knew how to say chicken, but she went for the cookies.

"Nyet, nyet," I corrected, *"Coo-peetsa."* She pulled a whole bird out of a pile of boiled chickens, hoisting it by the leg. She didn't hesitate at my awkwardness.

"Nyet, palovina." Half a chicken. She spun around and grabbed half a cold chicken, quickly wrapping it up in some heavy green paper. Breakfast in Siberia.

"Give me some of the cookies too, please."

She took another piece of paper and effortlessly rolled a cone the size of a small megaphone, filling it with a dozen star shaped shortbreads.

"Four carrots, two tomatoes, one bread, that's all!" Her aged fingers slid the small black beads of an abacus up and down the wooden shafts. The beads and shafts looked shiny and worn from countless tabulations.

"Three rubles and twenty kopecks." About four dollars. She was quick as a cash register.

She slowed her pace and smiled. The dark wrinkles on her face spoke of many Siberian seasons. Her eyes were a striking Caribbean light green. I thanked her, and gave her the money. She told me she'd grown the vegetables in her garden.

"*Shastleevway*," she said, wishing me good fortune. Her eyes sent a shimmer of warmth through me. Then she turned and hurriedly took the next person's order.

With my hands full of food, I sprinted the length of Shimonovsk Station, reaching my car a minute before the yellow flags fell.

Trans Siberia moved swiftly through the Khilok River Valley. I leaned against an open window frame and peered out across fields of wheat and grass to distant mountains. Haystacks resembling African huts dotted the Asian countryside. The white linen window curtains whipped near my face.

I turned to find my cabinmate, Pavel, behind me. We'd been sitting knee-to-knee for the last couple of days, armed with pens, paper, and a dictionary, trying to tell our life stories.

Pavel, in his late twenties, had brush-cut blonde hair combed straight back, and glacial blue eyes that never seemed to blink. He didn't speak English.

"*Eta ochen kraseevwee, da?*" It's very beautiful, yes?

"Yes, I really like the countryside."

I couldn't see enough of Siberia. I'd been staying awake into the early morning hours, just for a glimpse of an illuminated window, or the station lamps that shadowed travelers milling over the platform. Rail bridges and tunnels sparkled like cities in the darkness, surrounded by flood lights, fences, towers, and armed guards. The Mongolian border was just a hundred and fifty miles to the south.

"*Posmotree!*" Look, Pavel pointed to an older man walking along a dirt path near a small creek, carrying a fishing pole in one hand and a string of fish in the other. He wore an old suit, rubber boots, a shirt buttoned to the neck, and a small woven cap. His eyes were fixed straight ahead as if he didn't notice the train careening across the Soviet Union.

"That man knows a good life," Pavel yelled, his hair whipping in the wind. I started to say something just as an eastbound passenger train exploded past the open window, only six feet away. Instantly, the panorama turned into an avalanche of steel. We stepped back from the blast of hot air and noise.

"*Eta gromkey!*" That's loud, he yelled. The train disappeared abruptly. Pavel and I moved back to the open window and felt the rush of summer air against our faces.

We stood at the window for nearly an hour. Every ten or fifteen minutes a freight train blew by on the busy rail line. Pavel periodically disappeared to have a cigarette in the car's designated smoking room.

After years of Red Army paranoia, it seemed ironic that the first Russian I met was a soldier. Pavel had boarded the train two nights before, on his way home to Moscow after serving two years on the Chinese border. We didn't talk much that first morning, although I'd given him some carrots and bread to have with morning tea. His soft-spoken, unassuming manner made me comfortable. By the second day, we were talking for hours at a time. After struggling through a conversation, we'd sit back exhausted and look out the window, or read.

"I'll buy dinner tonight," Pavel insisted, waving his hand to dismiss any protest. We left for the dining car. Twenty-four doors separated our cabin from the train's restaurant car. The cars lurched and rolled, forcing a handhold as our feet tried to compensate for the motion.

I was sure I'd get something to eat with Pavel. The last few times I had ventured to the dining car by myself, I found the door locked, and my watch ticking in the wrong time zone. The waiter would hold his wristwatch up to the window and point at the dial shaking his head no.

Trans Siberia existed in its own tunnel of time, set to Moscow clocks. The train would roll into a town where the station clocks would say six o'clock in the morning, while train clocks pointed to midnight. Sometimes even the date confused me. At one end of the U.S.S.R., children were going to bed, and eleven time zones eastward, workers were pausing for mid morning tea break the next morning. I'd given up trying to figure out when the dining car would be open.

The first couple of nights on the train, I'd survived with the help of a short, rotund Russian woman who walked the corridors, calling out "*Koosheet! Koosheet! Xotitye koosheet?*" To eat! To eat! Do you want to eat? She carried a wire basket stacked with metal dishes of warm meat, potatoes, gravy, and brown bread. It cost fifty kopecks a plate, about seventy five cents.

The dining car hummed with Russian conversation, kitchen noise, and Soviet radio. A waiter with a small moustache and greasy hair seated Pavel and me at the last empty table. I studied the Cyrillic descriptions on the four page menu for a few minutes, while he and Pavel spoke.

"I'll have fish," I pointed to the word *reeba* on the second page.

"*Reeba nyet*," the waiter replied. No fish.

Pavel leaned across the table and placed his hand over the menu. "He says there is only one dinner."

That was simple. The menu was only a formality. Several minutes later, the waiter returned with a pitcher of ice water, cucumber and tomato salads, brown bread, and plates full of meat and potatoes out of a stew pot. I was reminded of the dinners my grandmother used to serve on her farm in the Sacramento Valley. Only the banging screen door and the scent of corn silage and alfalfa were missing.

"*Nraveetsa?*" Pavel wondered if I liked the dinner. "When you come to Moscow, I would like to take you out to one of my favorite restaurants."

The dining car parted a sea of green grass that spread into the valley. I was suprised by the abundance of agriculture in Siberia. Everyday, farms appeared. In many areas, men and women cut the tall grasses by hand, swinging long scythes in steady ponderous motions.

Earlier in the day, Pavel had attempted to describe the Soviet agricultural system to me. His appreciation for rural life reminded me of an old saying I'd heard, "Scratch a Russian, find a farmer."

With a ballpoint pen, he sketched two big boxes labeled *Sovxoz* and *Kolxoz*, two different kinds of government farms. He drew dozens of tiny stick farmers standing alongside tiny bushels of wheat with many arrows pointing toward the government box. But there also seemed to be a lot of stick farmers with ruble signs in their backyards, earned from small, private gardens.

I sketched Pavel an oversimplified view of our farm system. Independent, small stick farmers sent produce to the public market. Off to the side, a large banking box took a lot of the stick farmers' profit and sometimes the farm. The government box gave big farms extra money so they wouldn't grow anything. Pavel shook his head without understanding. I told him most Americans didn't understand it either.

Near the end of our meal, we were joined by two foreign travelers we'd met. A Japanese mountaineer, on his way to see the 20,000 foot Pamir Mountain Range in Soviet Central Asia, and a young Austrian on his way home after traveling across the United States.

The four of us spoke awkwardly, translating from English to German to Russian, and back again so everybody could understand. The Austrian's English amused me, especially when he talked about the bears in Yellowstone Park.

"Yahs, vee ver in dee park, and dee ranger said to look out fer dee beers. Dot deez beers vill come to us vit der noses to bite down. So vee ver much concerned to avoid dee beers."

He kept cocking one eye at my laughter. Pavel gave the German version of the "beer" story a serious listen. He spoke German as a second language.

"*Pa yeckalee.*" Let's go. The waiter had cleared the table and brought change for a ten ruble bill. The dining car was closed. After our dinner, Pavel and I sat on our bunks, enjoying the last of the light. A barefoot youngster pedaled an oversized bicycle along a dirt road near a cluster of village homes. Huge piles of firewood rivaled the size of some of the houses. Outside, the temperature was warm, but the massive wood piles foreshadowed a long winter.

The car steward knocked, asking if we wanted tea.

"*Dobray vyecher. Chaigh xotitye?*"

We both nodded. He used his hip to slide the door open, carrying tall glasses of hot black tea in ornate silver-handled glass holders. The steward, a pleasant man in his fifties, always wanted to know if everything was going okay for me.

"Tomorrow morning, at five o'clock, you get off the train at Irkutsk, right?" Pavel asked.

"*Da.* Five o'clock."

I didn't look forward to getting off the train. I was just getting used to my surroundings, and I had attached myself to Pavel. He was the first Russian I'd come to know, and he seemed to like me.

Since I first saw the Soviet coast emerging from the mists, I felt as if I were being swallowed by something huge. Four days and nights aboard the train, crossing a continent peppered by wooden villages with names like Chichatka, Amazar, and Gonzcha, and we were still thousands of miles east of Moscow. It took Amtrak three days to go coast to coast across America. I was a tiny speck in the belly of Siberia. But Pavel lived here. He knew the way out.

"I'd prefer to go on the train with you all the way to Moscow."

"That would be interesting," Pavel mused, "Then I could show you the Union. I would like that." Pavel referred to the Union in the same manner that Americans said, "the States."

Late in the evening, long after the city lights of Ulan Ude had faded behind the train, Pavel reached into his leather briefcase and pulled out a litre of Russian vodka. He set the bottle on the table along with a small loaf of brown bread. The red, white, and blue *Russkaya* label looked friendly.

"I bought this to celebrate coming home," he said. "It's been two years. And this time here with you is very good." He poured the vodka into our empty tea glasses after rinsing them out at the fountain in the corridor.

"*Nawsh druzhba!*" To our friendship.

"*Cherez fsyo vremya!*" For all time, I added.

I followed Pavel's lead, drinking the vodka in one motion, then eating a piece of brown bread. The patterned movement and steady eye contact made drinking more like a ritual than a casual cocktail. We sat back in our bunks and grinned at each other.

I tried to picture Pavel in his Soviet Army uniform, since he wore civilian clothes on the train. I thought of my cousins in their military uniforms, and told Pavel how strange it was to be sitting with a Soviet soldier after a lifetime of believing that people like him wanted to kill me.

"*Ya znaiyou eta choostva.*" He echoed that feeling. I was the first American he'd ever met.

"Do you think our countries will have a war someday?" I asked.

Pavel stared at me without blinking.

"No. I don't think there will be a war. It can't happen." He cupped his hands together, flexing both arms in an arm wrestling charade. "Our countries are like two strong men wondering who is strongest."

He smiled and leaned forward to pour another round.

Pavel sat up to the formica table and sketched an angry Russian Cossack with big teeth, glaring eyes, and a star on his fur cap. He grinned while drawing the character, then held it up for me to inspect.

"Perhaps this is what Americans think Russians look like?" Pavel sketched a second figure. A villainous Uncle Sam in a top hat of stars and stripes.

"And this is what Americans look like, yes?"

We both laughed.

Long after midnight, I remember Pavel painstakingly removing the vodka label from the empty bottle. Then he opened the window, letting in a blast of cold night air, and threw the bottle out somewhere between Selenginsk and Babushkin. He reached over and clasped my hand. We held on for a few seconds, looking at each other. There was nowhere else in the world I wanted to be at that moment. As the lights of another train flashed by, Pavel inscribed a personal wish to me on the back of the red, white, and blue label, between the brown glue stripes.

> "Zhon!
> I would very much like that we reminisce and travel across Russia and the Soviet Union. You have a long time to be here. I hope this isn't your last visit.
>
> Pavel"

Five o'clock in the morning came quickly. The conductor pried me from my bunk and carried my bags off the train in the darkness. Pavel sat up and shook my hand one last time, chuckling at my disoriented look. I hadn't slept very well. All night long, Siberian rail joints had clattered beneath my pillow like empty vodka bottles.

It's Warm in Siberia

C*haigh ili kofyay?"* Tea or coffee, asked the waitress. I stared down at an egg that was propped up and moving slightly on my plate.

"*Chaigh.*" I ordered the black tea. I drank half a dozen cups and ate some brown bread. I couldn't face the egg. I left it sitting on its porcelain stand, unshelled. My hangover needed to go for a walk.

I wandered into downtown Irkutsk and found an open air *reenoake*, a farmer's market. Several hundred shoppers browsed over the fresh produce, buying everything from beans and watermelons to meat pies and flowers. My clothes stuck to me in the heat. Maybe it was a combination of direct sun and nausea, but I felt panicky and disoriented. All I could hear was shoe leather scuffing on cement. No boom boxes, no shouts, no traffic, nothing, just loud shuffling feet. I was used to noisy American crowds.

I bought two apples from a farmer and retreated to a residential area of nineteenth century housing flats. Their carved and oiled wood exteriors gave the neighborhood a frontier elegance. The street was lined with large shade trees.

A little boy with a butch haircut, glasses, and a striped T-shirt, pushed a toy Soviet tank through a mud puddle while making motor sounds with his lips. Around another corner, a construction worker blasted away at the street with an air hammer that sounded like it was inside my head. I found a quiet city park.

The small sign looked insignificant fastened on the side of the old two-story building, facing down a narrow cement walkway. *Stolovaya*, a cafeteria for the people. A dozen wooden steps led up to a plain entrance that looked more like a fire exit. I watched a few people come and go before venturing in.

The door slammed behind me. A twenty-five-foot high faded yellow ceiling echoed the sharp clatter of banging dishes. The pungent smell of fried and boiled food permeated the dimly lit room. I waited in line behind a dozen people, mimicking the man in front of me when he reached for a tray.

My outstretched plate met with a violent splat. Fish, I thought. I didn't want to ask.

Behind the counter, an angry redhaired woman in a tall white hat looked like the seven-foot pontiff of St. Stolovaya. She moved with the ferocity of a logging camp cook, shaking her serving spoon, shouting orders in Russian to the kitchen help, slamming big kettles into place, just daring someone to complain. I quickly gathered up some bulgar and a bowl of borscht. With brown bread, tea, and a cheese crepe, lunch totaled seventy kopecks, about a dollar.

I spread out my dishes on an unoccupied table. A small squadron of flies showed up, but they sat politely off to the side of the plate and waited.

An anxious man in work clothes sat down across from me. After a few minutes, I initiated a conversation. The text-bookish phrase spilled from my lips as awkwardly as if I'd knocked over a glass of water on the table. "Hello there, by what profession are you occupied?" The man looked up surprised.

"*Yah rabotayou v mabyel zavod.*" He worked in a furniture factory. "You are a foreigner. Where do you come from?"

"California. I'm a tourist." I was glad I knew the word for furniture.

"California? You are a tourist and you eat here?" He made a sweep of the room with his bread hand.

"Right. I want to meet people. This is more interesting than the hotel."

The man grinned.

"Kak vas zavoot?" I asked him his name, another well rehearsed line.

"My name's Mosha."

He was on his lunch hour from a small factory. Most of the forty or so people surrounding us were workers, except for a colorfully dressed Gypsy woman wearing an abundance of silver jewelry. She sat in the corner talking to herself and taking occasional swipes at the air.

"What do you think of the Soviet Union?" Mosha asked.

That was a tough question since I'd been there less than a week, but I told him that three penny street car rides and hospitals without cash registers seemed impressive, but that I didn't really know much. Mosha seemed satisfied with my answer when I told him I was having a good time, despite a hangover.

He quizzed me on the cost of cars, bread, and apartments in the States, and weighed my replies against twenty kopeck Russian loaves and twelve ruble a month apartments. Mosha decided that he was better off living in the U.S.S.R. He bid me good day with a handshake and returned to work. I think he was still puzzled that I was there.

The lunch was good, except for the fish. I was having a problem with the fish. Maybe it was a bad day to force down a strong slimy substance. On the second bite, my lunch almost returned to the tray. I covered the fish with my napkin and slipped out the door.

I walked all day in ninety degree heat until my mouth felt like cotton and my feet ached. All I wanted was something cold. Behind some plate glass windows, I noticed some long open freezers. Rows of packages filled the freezer and the Russian word for ice cream, *morozhenoye*, was written on each wrapper.

Russian ice cream was famous. I'd read somewhere that in Moscow alone people ate 170 tons of ice cream a day, even in the winter.

I wondered if they would be ice cream sandwiches with

chocolate cookie backings? Vanilla? Maybe the green packages were mint. I didn't care what flavor it was, if it was cold. I picked one and held a handful of kopecks out to the cashier. She took a fifteen kopeck piece from my change.

I found a riverside bench and peeled open my first Russian ice cream bar. It had a strange coarse texture. I eyed the orange brick of ice cream thinking citrus, then took a large bite.

Fish! Salted fish!

I gagged, and spit it out on the sidewalk, then ran for a nearby drinking fountain to rinse the hake sherbet , or whatever it was, out of my mouth. The aftertaste was horrible.

Morozhenoye must have meant more than one thing. Or the Russians had one that Baskin-Robbins didn't. A closer review of the orange wrapper revealed illustrations of little fish jumping around the word *moriyah,* meaning the sea. It turned out to be frozen fish paste for cooking.

I walked back over to the park bench and found a dog licking the mess off the sidewalk. Most dogs would have rolled in something that repulsive. I still had the orange wrapper and its contents in my hand.

"*Idtee soudah sabachka.*" Here little dog.

The scrubby wire haired mutt finished off the fish paste.

A splash caught my attention. Beneath the frigid waters of Lake Baikal, I saw the milky white form of a swimmer. He burst to the surface with a scream, thrashing madly to keep his muscles and joints from seizing in the cold. He swam farther out into the lake, then paused to tread water and look back at the beach. He noticed me sitting on the rocky outcropping and yelled in Russian, "Come swimming! For your health!"

I just waved to him and shrugged my shoulders. He dove underwater again. A faint haze hung in the air, distorting the pine forested mountains on the far shore. Lake Baikal was far from the encapsulated tensions of tiny train compartments and crowded city streets. I enjoyed the quiet even though my ears were still ringing from the roar of the hydro-foil.

"*Zdarovaya! Zdarovaya!*" The swimmer was persistent. "*Xaroshaya voda!*" He was still yelling about health and good water.

I waved at him a second time and shouted a polite refusal. Two women walked nearby and I felt self conscious yelling at the lake in Russian. The swimmer headed for shore.

I knew the cold water would feel invigorating. It was a lousy day to be wearing thick black corduroy pants. I wished I'd brought shorts and a towel. Baikal was the Grand Canyon of Russia, the deepest lake in the world.

Siberia was full of surprises. Aboard the public ferry, some of the passengers appeared to be on a tropical vacation, wearing colorful short-sleeved shirts, sandals, dark glasses, and carrying cameras. It was a Soviet national holiday, and the public pier had been jammed with people that morning. I'd stood in line for more than two hours to buy my ticket, and from my place in line, had seen the tourist boat arrive, load its passengers, and depart without delay—no lines, no wait, and no Soviet passengers.

"Come here! Come here!" The swimmer was vigorously drying off, shouting and motioning for me to join him. His persistence made me wary, but I climbed off the rock and walked down the beach to see what he wanted.

"You are a foreigner? Yes?" He eagerly thrust out his cold hand to mine.

He talked so rapidly that my Russian was rendered useless. I guessed that he was about thirty-five. He was short, almost elfin, with twinkling dark eyes and large ears. He tried to describe with gestures what I might miss from his vigorous speech. My apprehensions suddenly disappeared. I liked this man. I told him where I was from.

"*Amerikanetz!*" he exclaimed, pumping my arm vigorously. "Good to meet you. Very good." He continued his friendly tirade of words. At best, I was on the outer edge of deciphering his rapid-fire speech, but I nodded eagerly, laughed, and pretended I understood everything.

"Where is your group?" he asked. "What, no group? You're alone? Very good! Very good! An American traveler alone in Russia! And you speak Russian." His excitement grew. Then a serious expression froze his face and he reached for my elbow. "You are the first American I have met. But do not be afraid. I am not a communist!"

I burst out laughing. He paused with an inquisitive look, then shook my hand for the third time, and introduced himself as Anatoly. I asked him to speak more slowly. He tried, but his runaway energy was just redirected into gestures as he simultaneously buttoned his shirt, put on his shoes, and carried on two conversations, one describing the natural wonders of Lake Baikal, the other about a school he attended in Irkutsk.

Anatoly stopped his monologue abruptly, pointed into the hills, and said, "Come to my house. Please, be my guest."

When I said yes, his raving reached a new level of excitement. A moment of doubt surfaced and I wondered if Anatoly was a lunatic. But as we walked together, I became comfortable with him. He managed to speak more slowly and simply, although his urgency remained.

We walked through the village of Listvanka, following a rutted dirt road into the hills far above the lake. The steep green landscape reminded me of the inland hills of Northern California. Roughly fenced yards and little wooden homes along the dirt road could easily be the wooded neighborhoods of rural Humboldt or Mendocino County.

About 200 feet ahead of us, an older woman in a yellow and black polka dot print dress stood in front of the gate to a small house. She waved and quickly disappeared behind a high wooden fence.

"That's my mother," Anatoly said, as we neared the blue and white house.

Before following him through the gate, I stopped and looked

back down the little valley to the peaked roofs of Listvanka, and beyond to Lake Baikal. The breeze rustled trees and hillside grasses, and a large shrub hung over the fence, spilling a brilliant display of pink blossoms from the yard.

I walked along a path of boards and ducked my head to enter a lopsided pantry. The floor was tilted, the ceiling slanted, and trapezoidal window frames appeared to float lazily in the walls. I doubted that a plumb bob or level had been consulted in the construction of this room.

The aroma of fresh bread and the mustiness of old furniture greeted me. I noticed that the rest of the house followed more conventional parallel and perpendicular lines. Anatoly's mother stood with her back to us at the woodburning cook stove preparing a hot lunch. She turned for a moment to greet me with a warm smile and hello before resuming her work. She was slicing hot bread.

An older man had been relaxing at the kitchen table with a cigarette in hand, staring out a paned window into the vegetable and flower garden. He appeared to be in his mid-seventies. His strong face was scored by long, deep lines. Anatoly introduced me to his father. He stood up, shook my hand, and offered me a chair at the table next to him. His name was Anton.

I set my shoulder bag on the cracked linoleum floor. Anatoly bustled around, hanging up our coats, clearing off the table, and telling his parents how we'd met. During this brief account, Anton listened and nodded from behind his cigarette.

Anatoly's mother, Galina, walked between the stove and the table, delivering plates and bowls filled with food, and making sure that I was comfortable. In a matter of minutes, the table was covered with an enormous dinner.

Anton lifted the lid from a large yellow bowl and slowly enunciated the word for its contents. "*Pir-osh-ki*." He accented each syllable. "Very good to eat."

"I know about *piroshki*," I replied. "What kind are they?"

Anton grinned and looked at Galina and Anatoly. "This American knows about Russian food," he joked. "Yes?" He turned back to me. "Mushroom and cabbage. Do you know these other things?" He motioned to the various dishes covering the table.

My Russian language ability was limited, but food was a topic I knew. With a small ray of confidence I scanned the table. The homemade bread was still warm and closest to me. I pointed to it. "*Kleb.*" A plate of garden tomatoes and cucumbers, "*pomidori e ogurtzi.*" A bowl of sour cream, "*smyetana.*" The cabbage soup, "*shchi.*" The cheese, "*sear.*" Butter, "*maslo.*" I came to the last plate, fish, "*reeba.*" I had passed the test. Anatoly slapped my shoulder. Galina's round face broke into a smile. She insisted that we eat right away before the dinner got cold, but Anton interrupted her.

"Wait. You are the first American to come to our house. You speak to us in Russian, you know of our food, and today is a holiday. First, a drink."

Anton snapped his index finger to his throat, a Russian gesture which indicates the intent to share a drink. He rustled around in a cupboard behind his chair and came up with a bottle of dry red wine from the Georgian Republic. Anatoly filled three water glasses. Galina didn't drink.

Anton picked up his glass. With a resolute voice he toasted to health, "*na zdarovaya!*" Anatoly and I, holding our glasses up, repeated the phrase. I put the glass to my nose, swirled the wine to release its bouquet, and washed a small sip over my tongue. I became aware that Anatoly and his father were both watching me anxiously. Their empty glasses were already on the table. This was not the California wine country, it was Siberia. I gulped down the Georgian red, then set the glass on the table with theirs. They looked relieved.

When we started lunch, Galina hovered over my plate like an owl, prodding me to try more *piroshki*, more fish, more soup. Another cup of tea?

When I thought I could eat no more, she brought in three large bowls with different wild berries in each, a plate of cookies, and another pot of black tea. Anton picked up a cookie and dipped it in his tea.

"Many days I see foreigners at the lake," he said. "They walk in their groups and talk their own languages. Mostly Europeans and Japanese, a few Americans. But you are the first foreigner to come to my house."

Across the table from where I sat, the multi-paned window looked out onto a flower garden abundant with pink cosmos and colorful sweetpeas. The entire garden was in bloom. As I ate blackberries and sour cream, I thought about the tourists I had seen that morning who had purchased the expensive tickets to avoid all the people. What were they doing now? What would be their impressions of Lake Baikal? "... Lake Baikal contains 20% of the world's fresh water supply ... is over 5,000 feet deep and 350 miles long ..." I quickly returned to the sunlit kitchen.

I noticed an old black and white photograph on the wall behind Anatoly. The framed image was of Russian soldiers with Stalin standing in their midst.

"You are looking at this photograph? That's my father." He stood up and pressed his finger to the glass showing me a young officer with a straight back and a smooth boyish face. I glanced over at Anton, who appeared not to be listening. The garden view held his interest. His mind was elsewhere.

Anatoly continued, "I told you that I am not a communist, but my father is a communist. He was in the army when he was younger. World War II was a very hard time in Russia." Anatoly emphasized these last words. Anton's survival of four years of war on the Russian-German front as a field officer had probably put many of those deep lines in his face. I looked back to him. He sat motionless, a slow tumbling cloud of smoke rising from his cigarette. Images of horror crept up in my mind—the Siege of Leningrad, hundreds of thousands of people starving to death, the Defense of Stalingrad, more than a million lives lost in bitter street fighting during the winter. Those realities seemed a long way from the warm, quiet Siberian cottage.

I wanted to say something meaningful to Anton, but managed only a mundane question about how he liked Lake Baikal. He was silent for a moment, then replied that he enjoyed resting and being near the lake. "Here, at Lake Baikal, it is very quiet."

After we finished the tea and berries, Anatoly invited me to see the rest of the small house. A pantry, the large open rafter kitchen and sitting area, and a sardine can living room with a seven-foot ceiling. Anatoly led the way up a back staircase to the second-story bedroom.

On the stairs, I glanced at my watch and realized that the last ferry to Irkutsk was about to leave. Time had been a remote concern. A minor panic. Baikal Pier was three miles away. "Anatoly," I said pointing to my watch, "the last boat is in twenty minutes." Anatoly didn't flinch. He sat down on one of the three beds in the room. "No need to worry," he reassured me. "No problem. I too must go to Irkutsk tonight. I have a bus ticket, and I will take you on the bus with me." The bus wouldn't leave for another two hours. My panic retreated.

In one corner of the bedroom, I spotted a wooden *balalaika* leaning against a wall. I asked Anatoly if I could play it. "You play the *balalaika?*" I told him no, but that I played a guitar.

My fingers strummed the oddly tuned, triangular instrument. The music from the film Doctor Zhivago came to my mind. I plunked out a melody on the high string and found a simple pattern that kept the other two strings harmonious. My technique made the instrument sound more like a banjo.

"Come! I want you to play for my mother." Anatoly led me downstairs, through the lopsided pantry and into the fenced-in garden. Galina was sitting over a huge tub of freshly gathered mushrooms, cleaning and preparing them to preserve for the winter.

"Mother, listen! He plays the *balalaika!*" He found a seat for me on the porch, then proudly stepped back as if unveiling a new discovery.

Galina dropped her arms to her apron and squinted to see me in the sunlight. "You play the instrument?" she asked. I explained that I didn't, but that I played other stringed instruments. "Please play." The tone of her voice encouraged me.

I plunked away for several minutes, producing an American

folk melody. Galina and Anatoly listened, applauding when I was done. Anatoly said that his mother played the *balalaika*.

"Then you must play for me." I handed the vintage wooden instrument over to her. She wiped her hands dry on her apron before taking it. Galina held the *balalaika* like a dear friend, adjusted the tuning pegs, and strummed a traditional Russian song that brought the instrument's authentic sound to life. She began playing slowly, then increased the tempo with Slavic vigor until her right hand was a blur of sixteenth notes. The melody was a blending of folk simplicity, with a hint of oriental mystery.

As I sat and listened to Galina play the *balalaika,* I felt I was touching the heart of Russia.

It was then that I began to understand a word I had learned in the Russian language, which is not easily translated into English, and difficult for a foreign mind to fathom. It describes the Russians' deep-rooted affinity for the land on which they have lived for more than a millennium. The word is *"Rodina"*—the motherland.

With a grin of satisfaction, Galina struck a resounding chord that finished her song, and looked at me.

"Galina," I said, "Where did you learn to play music? You play so well."

She gently set the *balalaika* down in the grass, leaning its fretted neck against the house. "When I was six years old, I was given a *balaluika*." She reached into the tub of water and took out a large orange mushroom. "I learned to play by ear and from friends."

"That's how I learned," I replied. "No school, only in life."

She laughed, nodding at my remark. "That's very good to learn. Music and life."

Anatoly appeared with two large glasses of *kvas*, a Russian drink made from whole wheat bread fermented in water. When he told me it was *kvas,* my stomach took a turn. Two days before, I had stopped on an Irkutsk street corner after noticing several people with their noses to the sky, drinking an amber liquid that looked like apple juice. The vendor dipped a tall mug into a

100 gallon *kvas* tank on wheels, and I drank it down. The first gulp was shocking. Nothing in America resembles *kvas*. Its taste lingers between sour apple juice and stale sourdough. I vowed it would never pass my lips again.

I thanked Anatoly for the tall glass of *kvas* and looked down at the small particles of soggy brown bread floating in murky water. He lifted his glass. "To health!" I wasn't so sure.

"To friendship!" I replied, drinking it down.

It was delicious. I told him it was much better than the street vendor's. He wrinkled his face at the notion of a vendor's *kvas*, and pointed to his mother confidently. "She makes the best *kvas*."

Anton came out of the house to join us in the garden.

Anatoly took the empty glasses back in and quickly returned with his small bag of books and clothes. He pointed to my watch and said that we should start walking for Listvanka to meet the bus.

Galina set her mushrooms aside and handed Anatoly a large cloth bag filled with dozens of *piroshkis*, fresh cucumbers and tomatoes, cookies, and a container of berries. She kissed him on the cheek. Anton stood up, gripped my hand and wished me good fortune on my travels in Russia. He sat down again near a bush of sweetpeas and lit another cigarette.

I turned to Galina. She reached out both hands to me and held mine for a moment. She smiled, "Thank you for coming to our home. Good-bye."

"A big thanks to you," I said, "To life and music!"

"Yes. To life and music," she repeated happily.

Anatoly held the gate open for me, and the next moment we were walking side by side down the dirt road toward Lake Baikal. In a matter of hours we would be back in the city of Irkutsk. Along the road we met a stooped old man with a white beard who shuffled along muttering hellos to us. A few wispy clouds had gathered on the jagged mountainous horizon to the east, but the sky to the west remained clear as the sun began to drop behind the hills where Anatoly's house stood. We stopped for a few moments to feel the last rays of sunlight.

The whole problem started late in the afternoon, shortly after a young woman flagged down the bus and stole the driver's attention. She didn't look like a rural Siberian, with her long painted nails, elaborate make up, and high heels. I could see no houses or cars where she stood, only the forest and river.

The driver revved the engine and the crowded yellow bus was back on the road. His steel gray eyes darted back and forth between the highway and the young woman. He insisted that she sit in a strange little seat bolted down next to his. I kept watching his eyes reflected in the wide rearview mirror.

He seemed to be driving faster now. I would have felt better if he'd had both hands on the wheel, but he kept reaching under his seat into a rumpled paper bag and passing candies to the woman. He'd say something to her, and laugh at his own remarks. She seemed indifferent to his overtures, although she accepted the candy. He didn't offer any to me, or to the older woman next to me who had a bucket of berries tucked between her rubber boots.

I was returning to Irkutsk after a late afternoon swim in Lake Baikal. Since meeting Anatoly two days before, I'd regretted not diving into the lake. I returned to Baikal to swim in the freezing water. I was glad the rocks along the beach were heated by the sun. As the bus jostled along the highway, my fingers ran over the smooth, time-sculptured bone I'd found lying among some rocks on the lake bottom, ten feet beneath the surface.

About fifteen minutes down the road, the driver swerved the bus off the highway and onto a smaller road that cut through a forest. I was startled. I think everyone aboard the bus was surprised. The passengers had been pretty quiet, but as soon as the bus veered onto the other road, the buzz of conversation swelled. The driver kept stealing side glances at his pretty passenger.

This was supposed to be the same bus that Anatoly and I caught. Now we were headed in the opposite direction. What if we were going where foreigners weren't supposed to be? I wanted to get off.

Another bus was pulled over by the side of the road. The driver flagged us down and wanted to know what we were doing in this area. Our driver yelled back, "*Ladna,* everything's okay, don't worry about it." He slammed his window shut and we took off again. The forest opened up into fields. A few scattered buildings appeared in the distance. We whizzed by a pristine, white bus stop shelter where someone had used a wide paint brush to slop on the bold word, MONTANA, in English. Graffiti artists from Missoula or what? Maybe a San Francisco 49er fan.

I thought about asking the woman sitting next to me where we were going, but she didn't look very talkative. She was a big woman who stared resolutely straight ahead, never glancing at me or smiling. Her scarf was knotted tightly under her chin and she took up quite a bit of the seat. I was pressed up against the side of the bus.

"Irkutsk!" The bus driver announced.

Irkutsk maybe. I didn't recognize any of the streets or buildings. It was an old dilapidated section of town. Most of the passengers got off the bus and disappeared down the sidewalks. There seemed to be a lot of grumbling, as if people had ended up in the wrong location. The young woman got off the bus too, but she returned to her seat with a small travel bag. The driver seemed pleased. I began to suspect that he was taking her on personal errands.

My mistake was to stay on the bus, hoping to see a familiar landmark. But the only thing I recognized was the low sprawling skyline of Irkutsk as it disappeared to the east.

Next stop, I decided. We'd been back on the road about twenty minutes. Irkutsk city center lay far behind us. So I waited. And waited. The bus didn't stop. We drove straight into the Siberian countryside. The bus roared along, gobbling up the white lines as the driver continued to entertain his pretty blonde passenger. A road sign said "Angarsk, 40 km." The next city. The sun was ready to set.

I stood up and yelled over to the driver, motioning to a bus stop in the distance.

"*Sledooyoushe ostanovka.*" Next stop.

He looked up at me, surprised and distracted. So did the young woman. I got the immediate feeling that a Russian would have said that differently. The driver's glances ricocheted between the turnout and me standing beside him. The bus slammed to a stop. I jumped out and landed in the middle of Kansas somewhere. Shades of Dorothy and the Tin Man.

A straight highway disappeared over low hills and farmlands. The bus turned into a tiny puff of smoke beneath a heavy orange sunset.

I briefly admired the colorful ceramic tile designs that decorated the ornate bus stop shelter, but I didn't feel very optimistic about being stuck twenty-five miles out of Irkutsk at nightfall, surrounded by aggressive mosquitos. Across the road, I tried sticking my thumb out to hitchhike. A couple of cars went by, but I think I was observed as a curiosity.

After a while, two young men walked up from a distant farm. One man's face and hands were as dark as the earth. He wore shoes, but no socks, a small woven cap and work trousers held up by a length of rope. He carried the four-foot blade of a hand crosscut saw, without the handles. His friend was in levis, with a nylon windbreaker tied onto an orange backpack. I asked when the next bus came through, which prompted the usual question of where I was from.

"California," I replied.

The guy with the crosscut saw paused, adjusted his hat a little, and looked down at his feet. He glanced at his partner with a slight grin, as if to say, "This guy's putting us on."

"What are you doing out here?" he questioned. I was wondering the same thing.

"*Nepravelna avtoboos.*" The wrong bus. Another car went by. I stuck out my thumb. Rejected again.

The young man wearing the levis took off his backpack and laid it in the gravel. "*Shto eta takoy?*" He asked what I was doing with my thumb up in the air. He mimicked my roadside gesture as he spoke.

"Hitchhiking," I answered.

"Heeetch-haeekeeng?" he mimicked with awkward curiosity. I told him that in the States, if you stuck out your thumb you might get a ride. I didn't tell him that you might also get a bottle thrown at you.

The fellow with the saw blade stepped toward me with his weathered thumb in the air. He made an erasing motion with his other hand to nullify the protruding thumb.

"Here, is this." His hand flattened into a plane, with fingers tight together. He raised it chest high, then pumped up and down with a robotic motion as if patting a very tall dog on the head.

"Ah, hitchhiking in Siberia." I mimicked his pumping hand. He nodded, approving of my style. Another car sped by, unfazed by my Russian gesture. It didn't surprise me. All the cars zooming along were small Soviet compacts. Most had three or four people in them. I also realized that I didn't appear as a single rider, standing next to these two characters with a crosscut saw and a loaded backpack.

We stood around the better part of an hour, swatting mosquitos, talking, and watching the western horizon for the next bus. Drivers began switching on their headlights. I was surprised by my immediate rapport with both young men and their quick response to accommodate my level of Russian language. They spoke in simple terms, laughing and using their fingers to illustrate descriptions in the dust and gravel at our feet. Now, I was happy the bus had taken a different route, in spite of the mosquitos.

Another car whizzed by.

"Heeetch haeeekeeng." The fellow with the backpack tried out the word again, laughing at its strange sound and wiggling his thumb around.

Roadside entertainment.

As the night sky darkened, I gave up the notion of hitchhiking and decided that I'd eventually get back to Irkutsk if I stuck close to these two. The fellow with the cap worked as a laborer in a big *kolxoz* farm a few kilometers down the dirt road. His friend was a university student on summer vacation visiting friends in different areas of the country via the rail system. They were headed into Irkutsk to a store that evening.

Our conversation leapfrogged into an economic facts and figures exchange, over wages, rent, consumer items, and transportation. The student, who lived in the big Soviet oil city of Baku, asked me about the long lines of slow moving bumper-to-bumper commuter traffic in America that he'd seen on Soviet TV.

"This is true?" he asked, quite amazed.

"*Da.*" I told him that American news clips showed long lines of Soviet shoppers standing motionless, waiting to buy food and consumer items. Our rural Siberian bus stop summit meeting also unearthed the fact that for the same amount of money, a Soviet teenager could either buy one levi outfit or travel across the country by rail five or six times. On the other hand, an American could buy one train ticket across the U.S., or half a dozen levi outfits. That explained why denim jeans fluttered like national flags from American clothes lines and ten million travelers rode the Soviet rail system everyday.

"*Avtoboos!*" We spotted the running lights of an approaching bus. I pulled a few kopecks out of my pocket for the fare, but the man with the sawblade and hemp rope belt insisted on buying the tickets. We sat in the rear of the crowded bus. The lights of Irkutsk soon appeared to the east, a jewel in the midst of Siberian darkness.

Irkutsk was a quiet city at night. Little traffic and few people. I strolled through one of the old residential areas, along Gorky Street, feeling the cracks of an uneven sidewalk beneath my feet. The air was warm and still. Large, deciduous trees veiled amber street lamps, casting long shadows. The open alleyways smelled of cats.

Electric music drifted faintly in the distance, then disappeared. I thought the music came from a home stereo. I stopped to listen. Nothing. Several windows showed light. I walked again. The music appeared once more like an apparition, glancing off walls, gliding beneath still trees.

I turned down another street. Cymbals and drums sounded louder. The ghosting music reappeared and vanished several more times. I walked along the north bank of the Angara River and looked out across the wide expanse of dark water.

An open-air pavilion built on a narrow finger of land sparkled with flood lights, while a crowd danced to a Russian rock band. A cement footbridge led out to the small peninsula.

It took me a few minutes to figure out that the concert was free, after tentatively walking through the entrance with a ruble in hand, thinking that someone would stop me.

The music was good, but a loud crackle in the speakers made it sound like they were singing over rumpling tinfoil. About three hundred young people moved conservatively on the wooden dance floor offering sparse applause between numbers.

The band played three more songs, then, in one wave, the entire crowd exited the pavilion. It must have been rehearsed. Three hundred people don't disappear in sixty seconds without a sound. A group of six remained on the dance floor in front of the band. They were joking around and seemed more extroverted than the stoic crowd. The band returned for a strange two-song encore to the nearly empty pavilion. None of this made any sense to me.

When the band started to break down their gear, I hopped up onto the side stage to talk with one of the guitar players. I asked him about *"popyoular plastinkies."* Popular records. With a surprised look, he rattled off the names of what sounded like a dozen characters from a Tolstoy novel.

His attention was distracted by the equipment teardown and other musicians. I had trouble grasping what he said, but he kept talking. We did manage to communicate a few shared images. In California or Siberia, rock and roll was rock and roll, a guitar was a guitar, and Lennon had rocked the world.

The concert stragglers wandered over and clustered around until the guitarist excused himself to help the other musicians who worked under the lights putting gear away.

"*Vwee Americanetz?*" It came more as a confirmation than a question. Half a dozen hands reached out to meet me. I felt like I was being pounced on. The group introduced themselves with a blur of names. They were all college students. A few of the guys had obviously been drinking.

I planned to wait around and talk some more with the musicians, but the students insisted I join them. No refusals. One reached for my shoulder bag and slung it over his arm. A young woman took my right arm and a fellow called Sergei gripped my left arm. Off we went, out of the pavilion into the night, a cluster of seven. They laughed and made loud proclamations between a barrage of questions directed my way. I felt caught in a human riptide with no idea where we were headed.

"*Egraesh guitar?*" Do you play guitar, the young woman named Katya asked. She carried a cheap, flat top guitar slung over her back like a rifle, held in place by a length of rope.

"*Da.*"

The whole group immediately stopped. The guitar was thrust into my hands and they huddled in front of me, leaning on each other's shoulders, waiting expectantly. I sang "Dark Hollow," an old country tune. They loved it. They would have loved anything sung in English.

After the song, we moved on. No one would let me carry anything. They all bunched together as before and we continued over the cement footbridge toward downtown Irkutsk. I wasn't used to such close physical contact in a group of people. Even my long-time friends moved at elbow's distance, except for greetings. Here, I'd noticed young women strolling together holding hands. Mothers and daughters too. At one chess match in the park, two men casually rested their arms on a friend's shoulder while watching the game. I liked the friendly intimacy.

A night policeman in a long gray coat walked his beat along the promenade.

"Shh, shh," Sergei hissed. Everyone hushed into giggles and suppressed snorts of laughter. One of the young men, Serioza, broke off and stopped to talk with the policeman for a few minutes. Boris (pronounced Bor-eese), a big husky guy, kept trying to get his drunken arm around me. Sergei and Katya reprimanded him.

We turned up Karl Marx Street, walking as a great twelve-legged spider. I was curious where we were headed.

"*Ne deleko*," Sergei said, not very far.

We caroused along dark cobbled alleys and up a side street to a small dimly lit park sandwiched between several four- and five-story apartment buildings. Eleven o'clock at night in Siberia and everyone wore short sleeved shirts.

Serioza showed up with two more friends and another guitar. He continued quickly across the park and through the double doors of one of the apartment buildings. He returned with a bottle of vodka and two water glasses. Boris kept trying to slide up next to me, reaching out with his big friendly paws and slurred phrases.

Sergei's cheekbones were wide and prominent, hinting at Cossack ancestry. "Zhon," he said urgently, his tone riddled with anxiety. "What do American people think about Soviet Union? About war?"

"American people don't want war."

"We don't want war either."

"Only friendship," Serioza insisted.

Their urgency sent shivers across my shoulders. My neck felt hot. "Would America drop the bomb a third time?" Their question stopped me. I'd always wondered who might drop it first.

Our sudden lunge at world concern sent us on a depressing tumble. Everyone felt nervous living in the crosshairs of electronic guidance systems. I'd had the same conversations with friends at home.

"Tell people in America we Soviet people want peace. Peace and friendship!" Katya's voice rang with emotion.

A chorus of agreement echoed her statement. Serioza opened the bottle of vodka and poured a four or five ounce shot in each, handing them to Sergei and me.

"*Mir.*" Peace. We raised our glasses. It was a long way to the bottom. I grimaced a little from the taste, remembering the last night on the train with Pavel. A shower of sparks rose in my head. Everyone toasted to peace. Everyone, but Boris. I knew he wanted peace too, but I could hear him vomiting in the bushes. A small swig of vodka remained. I was the honored guest.

Sergei handed me a guitar and picked up the other one. He sang a Russian ballad. A chorus of voices joined in on what must have been a traditional tune. I accompanied them with a running arpeggio of melody. They asked me to play a song.

I strummed a fast tempo ska beat from a song I'd written in Jamaica. Now in Siberia, the chameleon rhythm took on the guise of a Slavic backbeat. Everyone clapped hands. Sergei and the others phonetically mimicked the chorus line with me. They didn't know what they were singing, but they hummed over the rhythm. "Every living day, we must find a way, to better this life we're livin' in."

We played songs until after midnight. The music had lifted our mood. Boris tried awkwardly to relate to me by periodically grabbing the guitar neck. Each time, Katya patiently led him away and talked with him. He'd nod agreeably then return. I noticed that few lights remained on in the surrounding apartments, but no one had thrown their shoe at us for playing music.

"Zhon," Sergei tapped his watch. "It's getting late. Katya and I will walk you to the hotel." They wanted to meet me the next night but I had train tickets for five a.m. at Irkutsk Station. After an enthusiastic round of handshakes, good lucks, and good-byes from the rest of the group, we headed out of the park. Boris decided to accompany us.

The four of us locked arms and set off down deserted sidewalks. I thought the world was a fine place at that moment. The vodka left me feeling warm and lightheaded.

We passed beneath the continuous shadow of large trees. I wondered if the city had been built around the forest. When we reached the hotel, Katya and Sergei wished me a peaceful night. "*Spakoine noche.*" Boris mumbled something and shook my hand with what felt like a pair of vice grips. I started for the dark hotel.

I was about halfway across the parking lot when I heard footsteps running toward me. I turned and was blindsided by a flying tackle and drunken laughter. Boris had returned.

"Boris, *nyet*." I tried to wiggle free of his grip, but he'd gotten both arms around me in a wrist lock. I looked around, hoping that Katya or Sergei would come out of the shadows to save me, but they were nowhere in sight. Boris tightened his grip and dug in with his feet, the whole time laughing and repeating, "Zhon, let's go to my home. You will be my guest."

I tried to refuse, but my head spun a bit from the vodka. Boris and I stumbled around out in the parking lot until my resistance disintegrated into laughter. We were a fine pair. I agreed to visit his home. Boris was ecstatic. It was about one o'clock in the morning. We headed off arm in arm.

Boris lived about ten blocks from the hotel. We turned off the main street down a dark, unpaved alley. Cats darted around in the shadows, ducking behind a row of trash cans. At the end of the alley, an enormous hardwood tree loomed over the back section of an old, two-story green house.

He fumbled with a key, opened the door and ushered me into a small three-room flat, an addition onto the back of the big house. Boris told me his wife had gone to visit her mother for the week. He slid a chair over for me to sit on.

The apartment was untidy, but not a disaster. An entrance pantry led into the living room which tripled as the bedroom and dining room. A small kitchen and bathroom completed the apartment. Boxy wood cabinets reached to the tall ceiling, holding books, a television set, stereo, and clothes.

Boris staggered around, knocking into the chairs, trying to be a graceful host. I had difficulty understanding much of what he rambled on about. Slurred Russian was impossible for me.

"*Eta maya zhena*." Boris flapped a color photograph of his wife in front of me. The print was faded but I could make out the pleasant face of a young woman in a straight dress, standing in a park. I thanked Boris for showing me the photo. He hurried across the room and fished out a 10-inch stack of photographs from a drawer. I suddenly felt very tired. I looked at a dozen of the photos before giving up.

"*Spasiba.*" I told Boris thank you but that I had to go. I stood up.

"*Nyet, Zhon!*" He grabbed at me, laughing, and insisting that I be his overnight guest.

I moved toward the door but he held on to me. I tried to explain that I had to go back to the hotel. I was supposed to get up in less than three hours. Boris nodded eagerly, then ran to the icebox and came back with a withered apple the size of a small plum. I thanked him and put it in my pocket. When I got to the door, Boris leaped in front of me and latched it shut with a hook. Then he grabbed me around the shoulders, laughing, insisting I stay the night.

My humor began to wear thin. He was obsessively interested that I be his guest for the night. Was he gay? Or maybe he collected tourists in his freezer. My thread of hope was that he did have a wife, and some very nice friends.

Boris didn't release his grip. I wanted to get out of there. We waltzed around the living room awkwardly until I pried him off. I went for the door, and knocked the latch open.

Boris grabbed me from behind pinning my arms as I dragged him a few steps outside.

Russian hospitality had me in a bearhug at two o'clock in the morning in a dark alley in Siberia.

No matter what I said, he wouldn't let me go. I thought he'd finally relent. But he was just playing with me, laughing himself into oblivion.

My humor was gone. Textbook unpleasantries weren't working. "Boris, I must go now." "Boris, this does not appeal to me." "I am not happy with this situation, Boris."

I wanted to say, "Hey gorilla breath, get your frigging meathooks off me or I'll give ya one in the eye!" I thought I'd have to punch my way out of his grip, although making him angry seemed a bad idea. He wasn't acting mean at all. To him, it was funny.

Okay," I said, "I'll be your guest." I turned to walk back toward the open door. Boris was pleased. He dropped his grip and told me how happy he was. Now or never. I broke away down the dark alley. I could hear heavy footsteps after me. "Zhon! Zhon!"

I hit the street and broke into a sprint under dark overhanging trees. Behind me I heard Boris's forlorn voice echoing through the streets. "Zhon! Zhon!" He sounded hurt and sad. Maybe even lonely. But I kept running.

A Long Way to Perm

A young boy huddled under a blanket in the opposite bunk. He held both legs tightly against his chest and stared at me. I sat up shaking my head. He'd boarded the train while I was asleep.

"*Dobray ootrum.*"

He responded quietly to my sleepy greeting, but looked worried. I glanced at my watch. I'd slept about three hours since a pre-dawn departure from Irkutsk Station. I flopped back down on my pillow and stared up at the formica bottom of the upper bunk.

I had been dreaming about an enormous, winged dragon with crimson eyes and shimmering scales rising out of the Pacific Ocean. The creature pursued me in a nightmarish chase. I had been so relieved to wake and find myself safely out in the middle of Siberia. The rhythmic passing of rails soothed my nerves. I wondered if I'd thrashed around or called out while fleeing the nightmare.

I looked over at the boy again. He looked quickly away and focused his attention out the window as we rolled to a stop at Cheremkhova Station.

As the morning progressed, I managed to pry a little information out of my reluctant 14-year-old roommate. He was Erik from the city of Usol'ye Sibirskoe, along the Angara River. His mother and father had sent him off to visit his grandparents for a couple of weeks of summer vacation. The grandparents lived in Western

Siberia near the city of Tomsk, nine hundred miles down the tracks.

I set up my Russian scrabble board on the table between us. The checkered game board and small wooden Cyrillic letters quickly absorbed his interest. I simplified the rules and it took just a few turns for Erik to master the concept of intersected spellings and double point scores. Then he stomped me three games in a row. With his new confidence, Erik relaxed and became more talkative. We shared a glass of tea.

"Erik," I asked, "May I buy you lunch in the dining car?" He looked down at a sack on the floor, then back at me with a shy expression.

"Nyet, spasiba." He thanked me, but said his mother had made him a lot of food for the trip. I left unescorted for the restaurant car.

When I returned to the cabin after lunch, Erik sat up expectantly and smiled. He closed his book. I noticed a picture of a dog on the cover.

"Do you want to play the game?" His anxious expression made me chuckle. He'd waited politely until I looked settled before asking me. I set up the Scrabble board. Erik turned all the wooden letters face down with his long slender fingers and eagerly selected a dozen tiles. He looked like a China doll with expressive, dark eyes cast in porcelain skin. His lower lip always stuck out a little.

The train creaked to a stop in the small town of Zima. I recognized the name of this tiny Siberian hamlet located near the childhood home of Yevgeny Yevtushenko, the Russian poet. It was no different than any of the other small station stops I'd seen, but Yevtushenko's writings had given me a glimpse of life here.

Barefoot boys at the fishing hole with pockets full of bread; Uncle Andrei smelling of petrol and virgin forest, carrying the children on his shoulders; the farm houses, barns, and local bureaucrats. The same images that permeate rural America. I wondered if Erik had a favorite fishing hole.

We played Scrabble for another three hours while the train raced west across Siberia. Erik was a good teacher. He corrected my misspellings and taught me new words. I never did beat him. After four trouncings, I called for a break. Erik sat still for a moment, then pulled out a satchel of papers. He placed a photograph proudly on the table. It was a black and white portrait of a collie.

"That's my dog."

I picked it up and nodded approvingly. "What's his name?"

"Jake."

I wasn't ready for that . Maybe Fidovich or Comrade Spike, but Jake. I was supposed to be in Russia and here is this kid telling me his name is Erik and he's got a dog named Jake.

I pulled out a photograph of my own. "That's my dog," I countered, "named Pyos." *Pyos* meant watchdog in Russian.

"A Russian name?" he inquired with slight disbelief. He held the photo close and studied it. I didn't realize it then, but I was sitting next to a pint-sized dog expert.

Erik emptied his entire satchel of photographs and books out on the table. He was studying at a dog training school. He knew dogs inside out judging from the detailed charts of canine muscle structures and a book on the psychology of training and control. Erik hopped over to my bunk and sat next to me to show his photo collection. Scores of German shepherds and rottweilers were being put through their paces at a Siberian Dog Institute.

"That's me," Erik pointed at a little guy wearing an oversized padded dog attack suit with extra long, quilted arms. It transformed him into a stuffed scarecrow with a pea for a head. Another photo caught an attacking dog in mid-air, fangs bared, a second before contact.

While Erik and I traded dog stories, Trans Siberia whisked through taiga forest, across open meadow, and past village after village. We stopped at several small towns like Zima.

Erik noticed my fascination for the towns dotting the countryside. He dug through his cardboard suitcase and handed me a paperback guide. It was a station-by-station account of the entire rail journey from Vladivostok to Moscow, including some of the remote spurs that crossed into northern Siberia. Erik showed me

Taiga Station. He would meet a local train there to the city of Tomsk, where his grandparents lived. I thumbed ahead to see what the tracks had in store after Novosibirsk, but the pages were chewed in half and ripped out.

"Jake did that," Erik grinned. The city of Sverdlovsk and all of its railways lay in ruin, teethmarks everywhere.

He dug further into his travel supplies and pulled out a couple of plastic bags of food and a deck of playing cards.

"You want to play a game?" He held up the cards and spread out an offering of mom's homemade cookies and garden carrots. "An American game," he suggested.

What, Rummy? Hearts? Poker? Yeah, poker, we'll play for your cookies. They all seemed too complicated. Something simple. The game, "War" came to mind. But I hesitated to tell Erik the name. *Voynah,* "war" to Russians conjured an image of horror, not of games.

"I know a game." I improvised a new title: "*Shastleevway.*"

Good Fortune. Erik learned fast. We each won a couple of hands.

After the games, I gave Erik a photograph of my dog and her puppies and he gave me a photo of a young rottweiler he'd trained since it was a puppy.

Then I gave him three postcards from Humboldt County. One was of the commercial fishing fleet tied up in the bay at sunset, another of two people standing next to a giant redwood. The picture of the big tree brought a look of amazement to Erik's face, but it was the third card that shook him up. It was one of those joke postcards showing a huge rainbow trout lashed across the bed of a five-ton truck, a happy fisherman at the wheel. Erik stared at the card. He glanced up at me a couple of times, but held onto the card with both hands.

"*Eta shootka.*" That's a joke. I thought I'd better qualify the trick photograph. He laughed and shook his head.

"This is joke also?" He confidently held up the postcard of giant redwoods and tiny people.

"No, that's real," I said.

Erik looked uncertain as he glanced back and forth between the two cards before adding them to his satchel. He thanked me again and said that he'd put them up over his bed when he got home. A few moments later, he carefully removed a photograph from his collection.

"This is present too." His long fingers held the black and white glossy portrait of Jake.

When I got back to the cabin after dinner that evening, an older man and his young daughter had taken the two extra bunks in our compartment. Erik smiled a little, but he seemed reserved. The young girl was lying quietly on her upper bunk. I exchanged a greeting with her father who was wearing an old threadbare suit that had probably been stylish in Stalin's era. His leathery face accented his fierce eyes. Erik seemed intimidated by this deep-voiced man.

The man pulled out a bottle of vodka and snapped a finger to his throat. I joined him in a shot. He handed me a chunk of bread as a chaser. We talked a little, but his conversation became interrogative.

"How much does this cost?" he asked, roughly fingering my warm up suit. "Which is better, U.S. or U.S.S.R.?"

I had just had a lengthy bout of dialogue with a young Soviet fellow in the dining car and I didn't have the energy for another questioning exchange. I shrugged my shoulders.

"How much money do you make in work? How much does it cost to travel in Soviet Union?" The old man questioned me sharply. He seemed a little resentful. His hands looked coarse from hard physical labor. I was young. I had time and mobility to travel across Siberia.

His daughter murmured from the upper bunk, "No, Papa, no politics." He told her to hush.

Early the next morning, the train rolled to a halt at Mariinsk Station where the old man and his daughter would get off. He put his hand on my shoulder and offered me some morning bread. I think he'd been a little drunk the night before. We tossed back another shot of vodka before he left the cabin.

Erik and I traded addresses over morning tea. He got off at Taiga Station. We waved to each other as the train pulled out. He looked small standing all alone in front of the station with that lower lip stuck out and his cardboard suitcase full of dog books.

✧ ✧ ✧

A cool mist fell over Novosibirsk, Siberia's largest city. The Railway Station teemed with hundreds of travelers. Announcements boomed from a loudspeaker high overhead, flooding the station with echoes of train destinations, platform numbers, and departure times.

Outside, bass rumblings of diesel electric locomotives vibrated the air as several trains idled at the station. A uniformed porter driving a luggage jitney cursed and beeped his way through the throng of travelers.

"*Papa! Papa!*" A young woman's voice cried out. A slight figure in a white dress ran the length of the platform, clutching several packages in her hands.

"*Papa!*" Tears streamed from her eyes. An aged man emerged from a small crowd across the platform. He threw his arms open and hugged her with joy.

"*Papa! Ya shyeol ne tote platformoo,*" she cried, hugging him around the neck. She had gone to the wrong platform. They separated and admired each other for a moment. Her young rounded features contrasted with his toothless, gaunt unshaven face. Tears rolled down his cheeks too. She handed him a bag of food and a small parcel.

The conductor's yellow flag dropped. She threw her arms around his neck again. He kissed her cheeks, shuffled into his car and a moment later, his head emerged from an open window. He reached out to touch hands with her as his train slowly began to roll.

The smell of diesel smoke and wet asphalt lingered in the mist.

A wash of sunlight pierced the western clouds, transforming gray mists into subtle gold. The young woman in the white dress waved as her father's train disappeared out of Novosibirsk Station.

✧ ✧ ✧

After nearly a week of riding the rails westward, 24 hours a day, across Siberia, I began to suspect that Moscow was a mythical city, which people talked about but never reached.

An abandoned Orthodox church with onion domes rested in a green meadow on the far side of a river. It was surely the same church I'd seen the first day aboard the train in the Soviet Far East. Trans-Siberia was someone's cruel joke, an endless loop of track.

I was doomed to ride the rails eternally. It had seemed so innocent at first, all those travelers coming and going: Pavel, Erik, the Austrian, and the Japanese climber. They had all gotten off somewhere. I was still aboard. And now at Novosibirsk someone new had entered my cabin: a woman and her son. They didn't know my fate.

We started the day by partially ignoring each other after exchanging pleasantries. Tanya appeared to be in her twenties and Alek was her 220-volt, five-year-old son. They were traveling to the city of Perm on the western slope of the Ural Mountains. Tanya was quiet and reclusive, staring out the window a lot.

Following our afternoon tea break, Alek rounded up the remaining sugar cubes, each with a speeding train illustrated on its blue paper wrapper, and blatantly devoured them. Then he bounced on the bed and made wild animal sounds for some agonizing minutes.

"How far is Perm?" I asked.

"We'll arrive tomorrow morning," Tanya answered, abandoning her out of body experience. She attempted to quiet Alek, but he kept fidgeting, then ran out the door and down the corridor. I wondered if Tanya knew the connection between sugar and frantic anxiety.

Alek returned shortly, transforming the rhythmic quiet of the train compartment into a squeal fest. He'd brought two small friends in to play: a cute little girl in a yellow dress with ribbons in her blond curls and tiny red shoes, and her older brother, less impressive with his snot-stained shirt and loud, sharp laughter. He egged Alek on to new heights: the upper bunk.

I'm not sure what got to Tanya first, the continual sprawl of the Barabinskaya Steppe or Alek. He'd climbed to the top bunk, dangled, screamed, and hit the floor a dozen times. With false calm, Tanya ushered the other children out the door to their quarters. When she returned and instructed Alek to lie down, he obeyed. All was momentarily quiet in the Western Basin of Siberia.

I read for awhile, then drifted off into a nap. Sudden bursts of shellfire woke me. Alek blasted something out of the air with an umbrella. I found refuge in the dining car over a bowl of soup. We pulled into Barabinsk Station. Perm was still eight or nine hundred miles west.

When I returned to the cabin, Tanya looked up from a book.

"*Teakah.*" She put a finger to her lips, accenting the word "quiet," then pointed to the overhead bunk. Alek was sound asleep.

After some silence, Tanya said that Alek became hyperactive whenever they traveled. They were coming from her mother's house in Alma Ata, Kazakstan, after a two-week summer visit.

We tried to play Russian Scrabble, but the game progressed slowly. Tanya looked out the window between turns. It helped me that she was a daydreamer. I spelled *beriozka*, a 27-point word meaning birch tree.

Near the end of the game, Alek woke up. He hung his head over the bunk and smiled at me. I began to like him. He got up and played quietly on the floor with a green dump truck. I was just about to win the game when Alek backed his 10-wheel Kamaz rig up to the Scrabble board and began loading it up with the wooden Cyrillics. Tanya didn't protest. I watched my 27-point word drop into the truck, along with most of the other tiles.

Alek drove off, out the door and down the corridor. I looked over at Tanya, thinking she'd stop him, but she just sat there. I imagined Alek dumping the truckload of Cyrillics into the toilet and flushing them onto the tracks of Siberia. The thought of the bathroom made me squeamish. Since leaving Irkutsk, the condition had gradually deteriorated. Everything was always wet and a thin slime of muddy footprints had accumulated on the floor.

I caught up with Alek halfway down the carpeted corridor. He was crawling along on his hands and knees between people's feet being a diesel truck.

"Alek," I said gingerly, catching him by the seat of the pants, hoping he wouldn't scream when I took the tiles back. Alek giggled when he saw me. I was the big dumb guy who couldn't speak Russian very well.

I pointed at his dump truck load, "It's not possible for this game to go from our train room."

He laughed and chattered back at me in Russian. His voice sounded like an animated chipmunk, but he drove his dump truck back to the room.

After a brief station stop at Tatarsk, our wagon hostess brought the evening tea. Alek sat on his mother's lap and scooped up a few of the sugar cubes, then moved to a corner of the bunk to indulge in frantic nibbling.

"Do you want to eat?" Tanya asked me. I refused politely, but noticed mineral water, fruit, bread, and cookies in her food bag. There was a chicken in there too. I accepted the invitation for a homegrown, homemade dinner. We ordered more tea.

After the meal, Alek curled up next to Tanya and watched the flash of landscape pass by the cabin window. He grinned at me once. His smile had definite charm after a few moments of quiet. I think he liked me.

"Tanya," I asked, "is talking with me like speaking with a five-year-old child?"

"No, not a five-year-old," she answered, rolling her eyes to the ceiling and back, as if the answer were written up there. She was sparing me the laughter. "Mmmm, maybe a four-year-old."

"Oh."

Near midnight, Trans Siberia pulled into Omsk Station. Alek was sound asleep in the upper bunk, lying on his back with his mouth open, probably dreaming about forests of sugar cane.

Tanya asked if I wanted to go for a walk. A surprising number of people gathered outside Omsk Station for such a late evening. Young couples, elderly people, travelers, and a few off-duty soldiers walked along the cement platforms in the warm night air. The crowd was oddly silent. Some people ate ice cream bars purchased from a vendor. Others sat idly on benches beneath trees. We bought some ice cream and joined the quiet procession along the station platform.

Suddenly, a perfectly folded paper airplane glided out of a first class cabin window. Another followed. Then another. Two Oriental men with glasses peered out the window, laughing. A transformation took place.

An old man wearing a baggy suit stooped and picked up one of the airplanes. He threw it with the fascination of a young boy. A heavyset older woman picked it up and threw it again, laughing out loud. Others joined in. In a moment's time, half a dozen paper airplanes sailed through the air. Children, teenagers, and older people scampered and hobbled for a chance to throw a small airborne paper creation. Giggles and laughter bubbled from the crowd at Omsk Station.

Tanya pointed up at the stars. "Do you know that one?" "*Eta bolshoi myedvyed*," she identified it as the Big Bear.

"In America, we call it the Big Dipper."

I moved away from the lights for a better view of the stars. In the middle of Siberia, the same celestial images twinkled overhead as in America. Discovering Big Bear made me feel closer to my friends at home.

At seven o'clock the next morning, a grinding noise woke me. Alek, chewing up a stash of sugar cubes, smiled and tapped on the walls.

Outside, the city of Sverdlovsk rose into view. This was where the Tzar and his family had disappeared from the world. Perhaps Siberia had swallowed them too. As we whisked into the station, I saw a man without a nose waiting for a train.

After Sverdlovsk, we lost the "Big Sky." Trans Siberia ascended into the ancient Ural Mountains, divider of the European and Asian continents. The terrain changed from sprawling steppe and clumped deciduous forests to pine-covered mountains. The air cooled as we climbed. Ural rivers moved more swiftly than the meandering lowland waters.

The Ural Mountains had been chiseled by time into a low rounded range like the Appalachians. Small village homes lined the upper banks of a wide, green river that descended westward into European Russia.

Many of the homes were painted blue or yellow, with ornate white wooden window frames and roof trim. They stood like ornaments against the mountain greenery. Trans Siberia gained speed descending into Europe. Perm would be the first major station west of the Urals.

A strong smell interrupted my reverie of continental transformation. I'd forgotten about Alek. He'd been into Tanya's purse and was emptying a bottle of perfume on his head.

"Alek!" Tanya grabbed the container and scolded him, her voice trailing off in frustration. Alek rubbed his hair and quickly wiped his scented mitts across his shirt. The whole cabin reeked. Diesel fumes couldn't have been worse. I opened the window.

Tanya asked me if I'd watch Alek while she went down the hall to the tiny metal bathroom.

Alek and I alone? I cringed at the thought. What if he threw a tantrum? What if he wouldn't mind me? He could jabber circles around my Russian.

"Sure, no problem," I lied. Tanya looked at me for a moment.

"You want to do this, yes? I'll only be a few minutes."

All I had to do was make sure he didn't hurt himself or escape out the door. I remembered the pillow and bedding compartment under the bunk. Maybe I could coax him to climb in. I could shut the lid and sit on it until she returned.

"Sure, it's alright." Tanya left with her travel bag and I felt like a watch dog on duty.

Alek sat across from me grinning, his legs sticking out straight on the bunk. He looked innocent enough. After another cube, he shredded the back page of *Pravda*, a Soviet newspaper and blew spit all over his mother's bed.

"Alek," I cautioned, *"Tavaya mot etova nenraveetsa."* He grinned at my warning that his mother would not like this, then spit on the table and pasted the shredded bits of *Pravda* on the formica surface. He was kind of cute, in a way.

About fifteen minutes later, Tanya returned with her hair brushed neatly, wearing a fresh summer dress and makeup. "How was he?"

"He was a good boy," I replied, "but there's a little problem on the table there." I pointed at the bubbly saliva pool of shredded paper.

"Oh, Alek! I will tell your father." She mopped up the soggy *Pravda* creation with a hand towel. Alek got real quiet.

At Perm, Tanya's husband greeted her and Alek with flowers and kisses. I walked along the train platform looking at all the car windows. Nearly two hundred windows on one side of Trans Siberia, each one like a portrait: an old country babushka in a flowered scarf; tiny children pressing their fingers and faces against the glass like salamanders; a military officer with three gold insignias across his shoulder and a scowl on his face; a young couple with Soviet champagne on their table.

As Trans Siberia again moved westward, the Urals diminished from view. I returned to my room to find a Ukrainian railway worker moved in. We would share the compartment for a day and a night. And there would be others too, a young woman from Kirov, and another from Murmansk. Everyday for a week, 24 hours a day, Trans Siberian passengers lived in tiny cubicles, hurtling across steel rails on an ocean-sized land mass. Behind us lay nearly 5,000 miles of Siberian Asia. Our train raced into Russia's heartland. We'd finally made it to Perm, but Moscow was still very much a myth, nearly 900 miles to the West.

East of Moscow

The policeman waved his black and white baton at my Lada and I stopped. Brilliant gold foreign license plates made the car easy to spot. Soviets had black and white plates. I watched the officer approach in the side view mirror. I'd overshot the traffic tower by a hundred feet.

"*Zdrastvweetye?*" Where are you driving?

"Suzdal."

"From what country are you?" The policeman fixed unblinking eyes on me and leveled quick questions. His snappy manner was difficult for me to understand. He became visibly irritated that I was headed into the countryside and couldn't answer his questions.

"Give me your passport. Your travel visa. All your papers!"

Gulp. Dear Mom, please send warm clothes...

I handed him everything, the motel and camping vouchers, rail tickets, airplane tickets, my international driver's license, my whole identity. He disappeared inside the two-story glass control tower. All of a sudden, the Soviet State seemed ominous. I wondered if the policeman could just walk into his tower, punch a few buttons and know if I should be sitting there at that moment?

Arriving in Moscow aboard the Trans Siberian Express had been like stepping out of a time machine. The Soviet mega-city shocked me. Streets wide enough to land jumbo jets. pedestrians striding at a New York City pace, subway stations that looked like fine art museums, and at the epicenter stood the Kremlin. Limousines of military men and bureaucrats popped in and out of Spasskaya Tower on Red Square.

My pre-planned itinerary would route me through the Soviet capital several times. All the highways of the region pointed toward Moscow as if it were the ancient hub of a great spoked wheel. The city itself was circled by five highways that formed a series of rings from the Kremlin out to the suburbs.

It had taken me half the day just to get to the eastern edge of Moscow. Early in the morning, I rented a little Soviet-built Lada. Getting the car hadn't been a problem, just a few signatures and an American passport. A friendly Intourist agent smiled and held the keys out to me.

"Have a very good time. We will see you in two weeks."

"What about a map?"

"I'm sorry," he apologized, "but there are no highway maps. We are all out."

I drove away from the hotel in disbelief, nosing the Lada into the rush of Moscow traffic. After driving two hours on the wrong road, a policeman pulled me over and pointed me back toward Moscow. The patient, older man listened to my story, but offered only a sympathetic nod and pointed over the trees toward Southern Russia or the Indian Ocean, somewhere far over the horizon. Now I sat, waiting for clearance, my car pointing east on the Gorky Highway.

Footsteps in the gravel. With regimented formality, the policeman handed me my papers, offered a military salute, and motioned me forward to Suzdal. I wondered who he called, Intourist or the KGB?

Fifteen minutes later, the four-lane highway tapered into a narrow, two-way road traversing fields and colorful country villages. Every home had a TV antenna and an outhouse. People carried well water in buckets.

Scores of big trucks rumbled along the asphalt pavement, spewing black smoke out their stacks and holding back lines of darting passenger cars. The traffic was thick. I pulled out to pass a tractor-trailer rig. My heart pounded as I accelerated to 75 miles per hour. I was in Russia on the wrong side of the road, flying past a semi with another truck snarling toward me in a cloud of smoke. Everything seemed unpredictable. I slipped back into my lane, and slowed down to the 55 mile per hour Soviet speed limit.

After driving for an hour and a half, the road crossed a small river bending through a grove of birch trees where an outdoor grill and picnic area had attracted a crowd of motorists. It looked like an oasis from the two-lane carbon monoxide tube. My orange car added another shade to the M & M collection of red, green, yellow, and brown Soviet compacts parked in the turnout.

Two women in white aprons passively tended the grill in a grassy meadow alongside the highway. My taste buds blossomed at the skewers of beef and onion *shashleeks* barbecuing over a bed of hot coals. The older woman in white scraped the skewered meat and onions onto a paper plate and weighed it in grams on a scale. She used an abacus to figure the cost. I bought a bottle of beer, and found a vacant table.

Most of the people sitting around were families on summer vacation, or Moscovites with picnic lunches on a country drive. Some broad-shouldered young men arm wrestled with their sleeves rolled up. Their faces and forearms bulged behind locked hands and empty beer pitchers.

After lunch, I sat in the sun and tossed a few pebbles into the river. Some children splashed downstream near a camping area. All the tension from road traffic, policemen, the streets of Moscow, and a train trip without end started to let go. I lay back in the grass and closed my eyes. The highway sounds receded. Summer daydreams settled in against the babbling of children's voices and rush of water.

The road sign pointed north to Suzdal. I was surprised to see a dozen people hitchhiking wearing business suits or dresses. A few carried briefcases. It was 5:30 in the afternoon, on the northern edge of Vladimir, an industrial urban center 120 miles east of Moscow.

I swerved over and magnetized six potential riders.

"Suzdal!" I yelled out the window.

Immediately, all three doors opened, and the car filled with people and briefcases. I pulled away slowly. The small Soviet compact lost its pep with the extra seven hundred pounds aboard.

The city of Vladimir ended abruptly at a row of tall trees lining an irrigation ditch. Across the ditch, farmland spread into the distance.

I scanned all the new faces. They were a cheery group. "Thank God it's Friday" seemed to generate universal relief.

"I speak English very well," a heavily accented voice said from the back seat. Surprised, I glanced in my rearview mirror, then turned for a quick acknowledgement to the man in the middle who spoke. His wide smile supported a pair of thick, dark-rimmed glasses and a small wool sporting cap.

"That's great," I said. "I haven't met many Russians who speak English. Did you study at the University?"

"I speak English very well," he repeated. Everyone in the car snickered.

"Hmmm, I see. So you don't really speak English. You can't understand me. Right?" Another pause.

"Thank you very much," he laughed. "I speak English very well, ha ha ha."

We sailed along at 60 miles an hour surrounded by a sprawling sea of chocolate-dark soil, lush green field crops and a huge blue sky. Two tractors rambled along the horizon. A few billboards and it would look like the American Midwest. The Russian jibber jabber in the back seat made me feel relaxed, like I was part of a carpool with guys from work.

When I rented the car that morning, I didn't realize that I would be ferrying hitchhikers across Russian highways, or that hitchhiking was an acceptable form of Soviet transportation. I'd thumbed across the States a few times, but it seemed different in the U.S.S.R.

My first riders that day had been a young boy and his grandmother. She drew a map to her country home in case I wanted to stop for tea on my way back to Moscow. Then a stocky middle-aged truck driver climbed into the passenger seat, sporting a Charlie Chaplin moustache and a tweed suit. A small brown felt hat perched on his head as if it would only be there a minute.

And now I had a carload of Vladimir commuters. The hitchhiker in the front seat pulled out a one ruble bill.

"For gasoline."

I tried not to accept the money, but two more rubles came from the back seat.

"I have coupons for gas," I bargained, taking them from my shirt pocket and holding them up for proof. I waved coupons. My passengers waved rubles.

It was four against one. They insisted I take the gas money. "If not for gasoline, then we are buying your dinner for you." End of discussion.

Suzdal broke the northern landscape with a fairytale skyline of old world Russian architecture. Scores of bulbous onion domes dotted the turreted walls of monasteries and churches. The center dome of Sudzal's Kremlin billowed like a midnight blue hot air balloon drawn to a point. Golden stars and gilded orthodox crosses adorned the historic crown. The Kamenka River flowed through the town.

I dropped my passengers off in a quaint residential area of ornate wooden homes and narrow streets. Only a few thousand people lived in Suzdal.

When the comedian got out, he bent over and looked back inside the car with a grin on his face. "Thank you very much. I speak English very well. Good-bye."

A string of oncoming motorists flashed their headlights as a warning. The sun was shining and I was cruising about 20 miles per hour over the posted speed limit. So were most of the other drivers. My foot came off the gas instantly and I entered the speed trap.

A Soviet motorcycle policeman sat behind a bus stop shelter holding a metal radar device that looked like a vaporizer. He studied the readout, not noticing my foreign plates as I zoomed past.

The first few days on Soviet highways had been strange enough without all the motorists flashing their lights at me. I thought I was doing something wrong. American motorists flash you in the daylight if there's a wreck ahead, but that wasn't the case here. And the U.S.S.R. didn't operate by the Queen's rules, so I was sure I was on the right side of the road.

At one point, I stopped to see if something was visibly wrong with the car.

I noticed that every time lights flashed, a traffic cop would appear by the side of the road, either in a little gold and blue Dzhiguli with a red light on the roof, or on a green motorcycle. The police always looked ready to go after somebody, but I'd never seen a single ticket being written by the side of the road. I wondered if the patrolman behind the bus stop knew that every motorist on the road knew his proximity. After passing him, I felt confident and started speeding again, flashing my lights at oncoming cars.

I was driving south from Yaroslavl after spending a few days in the "Golden Ring" region where fifteenth century onion-domed churches and monasteries appeared in as great a numbers as the golden arches in California.

Another provincial village ahead. I slowed down to about forty. Scores of brightly painted little wooden homes stood alongside the tree-lined road. An old brick church lay in disrepair, surrounded by a yard of farm machinery.

Near the edge of town, a middle-aged woman wearing an apron over a geometric print dress stood at the side of the road and gestured for a ride. I pulled over and stopped under a big shade tree. She hurried over to the car and opened the back door.

"*Zdrastvweetye. Zdrastvweetye.* You are driving to Moscow?" She appeared anxious.

"Yes."

She turned back and motioned to someone. I wondered if this was one of those roadside ploys where a single woman hails a ride, then Uncle Petrov and his four companions with luggage come out from behind a bush.

"Please," the woman turned back to me, "my daughters must go to the train station in Moscow."

"Your daughters?"

Two girls around fourteen years old, dressed like small town teenagers from a 50's movie, carrying stuffed vinyl travel bags emerged from the shade.

"*Da.* Is this possible?"

"Of course," I said. I remembered the flat tire in my trunk. "But I might have to stop." I forgot the words for tire and air. The best I could do was a hand charade with an air leak sound, telling her that a soft circle needed repair.

"I understand. That's fine." She nodded and turned to give a hug to each of her girls. They slipped into the back seat, sticking close together, rolling the window down and giggling. Their mother reached her head in the open window, giving them one last hug and a kiss. "*Shastleevway.*" She said, as she backed away from the car.

I pulled out slowly, being ultra careful so the woman would realize what a safe driver I was and wouldn't worry. As we left the village, I glanced in my rear view mirror. Both girls waved out the back window. I tried to imagine a mother in her apron on California's Highway 101, flagging down motorists to take her teenage daughters into San Francisco so they could catch a train.

"What time does your train leave?"

Shy giggles bubbled from the backseat.

"This evening," one ventured, covering her mouth with her hand.

"*Xarasho.*" No problem. I paused. "Which city are you traveling to?"

"Novgorod. Our aunt and uncle live there." Giggles.

That was about the extent of our conversation.

A few kilometers down the road, I noticed a blue sign with a monkey wrench on it. I told the girls I had to stop to fix the tire. Two bashful faces nodded.

The repair shop was set back off the road in a grove of trees. About half a dozen cars sat in the parking lot, and a few people milled about. As soon as the shop foreman found out I was a foreigner, my problem became top priority. He took the tire and I went for a walk. The girls remained in the car.

The garage lacked computer diagnosis and digital balancing. But outside the office, a gravel path led into a large flower garden with white statues and benches. A lawn with shade trees was a nice place to wait out greasy problems.

A portly fellow with lively blue eyes walked up and introduced himself. He'd seen my foreign plates and wanted to know where I was from.

"Who's better, Americans or Russians? Ha, ha, ha. How do you like Soviet Union? As bad as you thought? Ha ha ha." His chatter bordered on a one-man conversation. He asked me questions then quickly filled in the answers with his funny little voice, all the while standing on one foot, then the other. His eyes never strayed from me though.

He was a physician from the city of Gorky. He and his wife and kids were on a three week camping trip, driving around in the northern provinces. He looked more American than I did with his blue levis, and sandy hair permed into tight little curls. I had on a pair of Russian sandals and a Soviet-made shirt.

"*Vwee znaiyetye Ruskie pisatseyalee?*" he asked, quizzing me on whether I knew Russian writers.

"*Da.* Chekov, Shukshin, and Yevtushenko," I replied.

"*Xarasho.*" The man from Gorky nodded, then held out his hand with four fingers proudly extended. He named his favorite American writers, bending each finger down as he spoke, "Mark

Tvain, Zhak Loandon, Hemeengvay...You like Faulkner?" he asked.

I'd never read a Faulkner novel, only his short stories. My reply brought a look of astonishment to the physician's rotund face. "What? You have not read the books of Villiam Faulkner? My friend, you have hole in your education. Ha, ha."

The garage foreman waved me toward the office. A certain form was missing. The bookkeeper fussed through desk drawers, piles of stacked papers, and under boxes, trying to find the right form. Customers came in to ask her questions, but she couldn't help them.

"Oh Mama!" She slumped back in her chair. "Today is only my second day at this work. Everything is difficult."

She finally came up with the proper form. I signed my name in five places and showed her my passport, visa, and driver's license. The shop had no change so I got a discount.

My two riders stood patiently alongside the car. The foreman in blue coveralls insisted on rolling the tire out to the car himself, and placing it in the trunk. When I pulled out, he and the book-keeper stood out front and waved good-bye.

By the time we reached Moscow, clouds had darkened the sky. Rain began to fall in sheets. The girls were grumbling about the weather.

I pulled over to get my windshield wipers out of the trunk.

Soviet wipers were in short supply. I'd been warned to take them off the car unless it was raining or they'd be stolen.

"Where do you want to go in Moscow?" I asked the girls, after jumping back in out of the rain.

"Vedehenka Metro. Do you know where that is?"

It was nearby. The underground metro would take them to the train station faster than an automobile and it only cost a nickel. They both thanked me several times for the ride, then popped open their umbrellas and hurried toward the subway station.

I stood in line to buy a drink from a vending machine called *"Gazirovannaya Voda."* For three kopecks, a customer received a tall glass of carbonated water. For another two kopecks, the machine added a creme soda flavoring. Each machine had its own glass—one glass—from which everyone drank.

The first time I tried to get a drink, I watched the carbonated water go down the drain, after the cup I had expected failed to appear. That was before I noticed the thick glass sitting upside down in a round opening.

Mimicking the person at the next machine, I pressed the glass down several times, activating a ring of water jets that sprayed the inside and the rim. I did this two or three times before placing the glass under the soda spigot and depositing my kopecks.

In every city where I bought a drink of water, from Irkutsk to Moscow, the glasses were never missing.

If Tamara had only turned on the headlights I wouldn't have felt so paranoid, even though we were hitting over sixty miles an hour in a residential neighborhood. The car bottomed out when we bounded across an intersection. I braced one hand against the dash board.

"What's the matter?" Tamara's voice sounded relaxed, as if we were waiting at a stop light.

"Slow down! You're making me really nervous," I repeated. It had been a real mistake to let this woman drive my car.

Tamara glanced over from behind her wire-rimmed glasses. My stiffened posture won some sympathy. "But this is how I always drive." She slowed down to fifty-five. A few minutes later, she turned onto the highway skirting Moscow. Her speeding didn't bother me so much on the open road. At least Soviet traffic law said headlights could be used on the highway at night. Motorists were supposed to drive with parking lights in the cities.

"Where are we going?" I asked. This wasn't the way to my

campground. She'd offered to drive me across the city so I wouldn't get lost in the winding maze. We certainly weren't going to look at any more war memorials or museums at this hour. Tamara kept both hands on the wheel and watched the road. She didn't talk much while driving.

"I'm taking a different road to your campground. We'll avoid the city. It will be simpler."

I'd met Tamara that afternoon on a park bench along the Moscow River. She walked by and asked me for the time. After staring at my watch for a few seconds, I came up with a somewhat correct Russian response for 4:40. Five o'clock, without twenty minutes.

She stood there for a second with a puzzled expression and asked me if I was from Estonia, or maybe Poland. My Russian wasn't authentic enough even for the time of day.

After a brief conversation, Tamara, who spoke some English, offered to show me around Moscow. I liked the possibility of a tour guide, but I wondered if someone wanted to know what I was doing driving around in Russia. Why not send a young woman to find out? I decided to not let that bother me. Even if she was an informer, it would be a cheap way to see Moscow. Intourist would have charged me twenty-five American dollars. But in retrospect, at least they wouldn't have tried to kill me in my rented car.

Tamara told me she was a member of Komsomol, the communist youth party. She asked a lot of questions, like why I had come to the U.S.S.R. alone, and was I a Republican or a Democrat? She'd never heard of a non-partisan independent voter.

She invited me to her parents' apartment for dinner. We rode a creaking elevator up to the seventh floor where a red vinyl covered door opened into the kitchen. Tamara's mother was a small, friendly woman. She wiped her hands on a towel before welcoming me to her home.

The apartment seemed large by Russian standards. Two bedrooms opened into a well furnished living room, crowded with a glass case of Chinese ceramics, a Central Asian wall hanging, an upright grand piano, some stuffed chairs, a couch, and glass doors that opened onto a balcony. Tamara made me a tape of underground Russian rock music on her Japanese cassette player.

Her family definitely had some advantages beyond average Soviet citizens. She had traveled in Hungary and Italy with a girlfriend and wore western jeans. I noticed a color brochure for Porsche pinned on the wall of her room.

Tamara was friendly and charming, but aloof. When talking about politics, she switched over to Russian and spoke very quickly, without much eye contact. I wondered if I was hearing party rhetoric. She obviously didn't care if I understood or not, although she had spoken in English when we were walking in downtown Moscow. She had pointed to the red banners that decorated buildings with party slogans like, "Glory to the People," and "Hard work builds Socialism."

"Reading these words everyday doesn't make me want to work harder, or feel like a better person," she said. "People don't pay any attention to these signs. I think they're not necessary."

Tamara seemed disenchanted with her work as a computer programmer, if that's what she really did. She told me she wanted to be a tour guide for English speaking groups. Before she could switch professions though, she owed the state four years of work in her field in exchange for her free education.

As I sat on the couch trying out her brother's electric guitar and sipping Cuban rum, the door from the kitchen slid open. A severe looking man walked in wearing a Soviet Army officer's uniform under a long trench coat. He didn't remove his gold braided hat but walked directly over to me without smiling. My year in military school made me jump up quickly in response to the uniform. Tamara's father reached his hand out and said something. I didn't listen. I was too preoccupied by his intensity.

"Pleased to meet you," I replied, wagging on the end of his grip. He nodded, turned, and left the room. I turned nervously to Tamara.

"What was that all about?"

"That was papa," Tamara said, grinning at my concern. "He

saw a foreigner's car downstairs and wondered who from another country would come to this apartment building. Then he found you in his home. You are the first foreigner to ever be in his home. And he welcomed you."

I thought he'd just given me five minutes to get out of town.

As we drove along the highway that night, a lighted, Soviet traffic control tower appeared in the distance. Trouble ahead. My nerves grated against my brain.

"Tamara, we can't go by that tower!" I pointed down the road. "My passport and driver's license are at the campsite."

"Don't worry." Tamara kept driving. She didn't seem to care.

"No, you don't understand. They'll stop the car. It has foreign plates!"

The tower was getting larger by the second. I could see a policeman sitting in the window. A foreigner without ID, heading out into the countryside at midnight, with a young communist woman.

"Turn around. We must!"

"Don't worry," she said.

I surrendered and slumped back in the seat. I wished I had never let her drive the car. None of this would be happening to me. She slowed fifty yards before the tower, then turned sharply off the highway onto another road.

"This road leads to your campsite," she said.

"Oh."

I felt a little stupid, but angry that she hadn't told me what was happening. How was I supposed to know? When Tamara stopped at the campground, she looked at her watch and told me she'd missed the last bus by five minutes.

"Can you give me a ride home?" she asked. "Or will it be too difficult to find your way back?"

I didn't believe her. It seemed absurd after driving me all the way here. She probably just wanted to drive the car again.

Moscow was a city of eight million people. Tamara lived on the far side of the urban center. It took me half an hour to drive back to her folk's apartment. This time, I memorized the route.

We pulled up under a street lamp and she started to write her address on a piece of paper so I could mail her a postcard from the States.

An older woman came running out of the darkness with a look of terror on her face. She was crying and holding herself with both arms across her chest. My first thought was rape. Tamara talked with her. The woman was having severe chest pains. She needed a hospital and my car was the only one in sight. Tamara opened the back door for her, then held her hand and talked quietly to her. We raced across the city, the woman sobbing in the back seat. She had vomited on herself. I rolled the window down for fresh air.

Now it was my turn to drive a hundred kilometers an hour through neighborhoods. I disobeyed the law and used headlights. The hospital looked vacant when we pulled up. Only a few lights were on.

"*Spasiba, spasiba bolshoi!*" The woman cried. Thank you, thank you very much! She opened the car door and ran down the sidewalk still holding her chest as she disappeared into the emergency room. A nurse was near the door.

"That's all we can do," Tamara said. "The doctors will take care of her. Let's go."

I made it back to the campsite at one o'clock in the morning and the gate was locked. A grumbling attendant finally came out in his nightshirt to open the padlock.

My nerves wouldn't let me go to sleep that night. I just stared at the walls of the tent cabin, watching insomnia theater replay the roller coaster ride, without headlights, and a desperate woman in the night.

One of Tamara's comments stayed with me. I had asked her if she was happy living in the Soviet Union.

"Am I happy with my life? No, not all the time. Sometimes I am really happy. But other times I'm not happy at all and I don't know why. I just feel sad. Tell me, are people happy all the time in America?"

Six White Geese

About twenty paces back from the roadside, two old women sat on a wooden bench beneath a shade tree. One woman flicked a long crooked switch at a small flock of white geese nibbling in the grass at her feet. The corrugated metal roof and split log gable of a house peeked over a weathered plank fence behind them. Tin buckets filled with apples and potatoes, placed near the base of the tree, were intended for motorists driving across the countryside toward Kalinin and Moscow.

When I got out of the car, the woman with the switch in her hand stood up slowly and shuffled across the grass to meet me. She wore a scarf over her head, a faded sweater, and rubber boots. Her neighbor nodded my way and walked down a dirt path toward a green and white house next door. All of the homes in the neighborhood had fences and large trees around them.

"*Zdrastvweetye.*" The small stooped *babushka* greeted me with the slow cadence of her country dialect. She had a face like a withered apple.

"Hello," I replied, "Did you grow these in your garden?"

"*Da. Vweerashivalee.*" She nodded with a proud smile. The deep lines in her face drew back into new patterns. She reached carefully into the mound of apples, brushing their shapes with her fingertips. She selected one and placed it in my hand. The firm, reddish-green apple smelled like a spring blossom. I was sure no pesticide had touched its skin.

"Very good apples. How much do they cost?"

"One ruble and fifty kopecks for all the apples." She held up her fingers to help illustrate their worth. They were the best apples I'd seen in Russia.

"*Da*, I'll buy all the apples."

"*Xotitye kartoshky tozhe?*" Do you want the potatoes too?

"No thank you." Twenty-five pounds of potatoes were not ideal for a light traveler.

The old woman looked at me inquisitively. She gestured for a bag. Obviously, I didn't get the bucket. I had to come up with a container.

My soft luggage shoulder bag looked like it would hold a lot of produce, so I dumped all my clothes into the trunk of the car. A packet of California poppy seeds tumbled out. A timely gift.

The old woman loaded apples into my travel bag one at a time. She held one firmly in front of me. I nodded appreciatively and helped her stuff the bag until it wouldn't shut.

We stood and talked for about ten minutes. Each time she made eye contact with me, my shoulders tingled. The inspiration came from standing in the Russian countryside buying produce from a dear *babushka* with transparent blue eyes.

"Here, I want you to have these." I handed her the seed packet. She studied the colorful graphics, unable to read the strange English description of contents. Her finger pointed to the golden flowers on the packet. "These?"

"*Da, da, da,*" I nodded my head. "In the spring, plant these in your garden soil. Then, during summer, beautiful flowers will grow—like they do in California."

"*Spasiba bolshoi.*" She looked appreciative. "Please wait."

The tiny woman picked up her switch and shuffled over to the geese that pecked in the grass. She chirped and hissed at the white birds and gently prodded them along the earthen path toward the front gate of her fenced yard. She gestured for me to follow. I walked slowly at the end of the procession. She herded the six geese through another gate made of small tree limbs nailed together.

"*Pazhalsta, idtee soodah,*" please come along. She pointed her long crooked switch along the side of the house toward the back yard. The dirt path was worn hard and smooth by many years of walking back and forth from the house to the garden. Ornately carved wooden window frames adorned her home. A glass vase filled with red and pink flowers stood against white lace curtains on one of the window sills. The house sloped into the ground.

Past the house, past a large, sheltered stack of split firewood, and beyond a small outhouse, we came to the garden and apple orchard. One section was entirely flowers. She waded into the waist-high patch of color.

"I want to give you some of my flowers. Perhaps you have a friend in Moscow?"

She cut a few daisies and handed them to me, then went slowly along the rows picking others and bunching them in one hand. Puffy clouds raced by overhead, alternately splashing the garden in sunlight and shadow. A well stood nearby, with a little roof over it, and a hand-cranked water bucket hung on a rope. The flower scents mixed with the sweet smell of grass from a nearby field where cows grazed. It was so quiet in the farmlands.

"Do you have a family?" I asked.

"*Da.* Two sons." She paused and looked across the flower patch. "They work in Moscow. My husband died in the war, many years ago. How do these look?" She changed the subject, holding up a mixed bouquet of white, purple and red flowers. "The weather becomes colder now. See, already frost makes them brown." I noticed a faint tinge of discoloration on a few flowers that she hadn't picked, but the ones for me looked perfect. I admired them, honored by the gift.

The old woman walked over to the edge of the garden where I stood, and placed her hand on my arm. I expected her to say something about weather or gardens.

"Your president is very rich man I think. Does he not understand people with little money? To bomb our land. Why is this a joke?" She looked at me intently, unblinking. Her bony hand rested on my arm. I couldn't respond. Even in the remote countryside, an old woman with six white geese feared for the world's future. She had lived through war. What could I say to her? She knew life better than I did. A foreign army had rolled through these fields and her village in the forties, on their way to Moscow and Kalinin. Tank tracks remained deeply rooted in people's memories.

"No war," she repeated, "*Ne voinah.*"

I asked if I could take her photograph, but she declined. She walked with me to my car and wished me a safe journey to Moscow. For the rest of the day, in every village I drove through, I saw her. She was the same person I saw bundled up, standing on street corners and in underground walkways, selling her flowers for a few kopecks to passers-by in the cities.

The highway to Moscow became a backdrop. I could only see the concern in the old woman's eyes when she spoke of war, the kindness in her face as she handed me the bouquet of flowers from her garden. I remembered her light touch on my arm, the gentle flicking of her switch at the six white geese.

My birthday was off to a bad start. The weather had cooled under a heavy drizzle and the campground's communal hot water system failed. After taking a cold shower on a cement floor, I walked shivering back to the tent cabin.

Then I noticed the flat tire. My cute little orange Lada didn't like me anymore. The previous day, a loud snap in the transmission finished off the reverse gear, leaving me with four speeds forward, and no options to back up. A traffic cop had fined me five rubles for not having my seatbelt fastened. I needed good news.

After fixing the flat in the rain, I decided to drive into Leningrad and take the hydro-foil ferry to Petrodvoretz, Peter the Great's Palace. I waited at the pier on the Neva River for an hour and a half, but the boat didn't come. A man with a fishing pole and no fish told me the ferries had stopped running because of winds and heavy rain. I decided to try the car.

I drove west through the streets of Leningrad, windshield wipers slapping back and forth, trying to follow a folded six-inch xeroxed map representing twenty square miles of old world, metropolitan sprawl. Like a spiderweb, the streets made abstract connections, winding between oddly shaped blocks of buildings intersected by scores of canals. American cities seemed like mathematical checkerboards compared to the jigsaw puzzle of Russian streets.

Some street signs in downtown Leningrad were fastened to the corners of buildings set back about thirty feet from the curb and often hidden behind large trees. I continued along main boulevards until I was off the map and into the intuitive zone. A flashing red light on the gas gauge signalled problems yet to come. I hadn't seen a gas station for a couple of days.

My downward spiral had started two days before when I started feeling sick and had a violent coughing spell in the periodical section of a library. Everyone in the room watched me try to escape out the door past an irate librarian who barred my passage. She made an example of me for not checking my shoulder bag at the front desk when I'd entered the place. I guess she thought I might be stealing magazines. My beet red complexion and hacking foreign accent won an instant apology, but I felt sick and degraded when I stepped back outside into the rain.

Half an hour later, I'd found an *aptyeka*, a Russian drug store. I hoped to find something on the shelf for my cough, but the only shelves were metal racks filled with dried herbs. Being sick on the far side of the planet worried me. The *aptyeka* operated on descriptions, not prescriptions.

"I have a cough," I told the young woman behind the counter, "and my head is hot and crazy."

She asked questions that I couldn't understand, grinning and raising her eyebrows at a co-worker, then handed me some little pink pills, some white ones, and a bottle of eucalyptus cough medicine, for thirty-five kopecks.

"Two of these every four hours," she said, holding one of the pills up in front of my nose. "And one of these three times a day. Do you understand?"

"Yes." I should have written it down. By the time I got back to the camp area, I forgot which pill was which, so I took four, every four hours and ended up feeling dizzy. But the cough and fever went away.

Finally, I spotted several gas pumps secluded behind a row of small trees. Five or six cars sat in line at the low-octane pumps. When I rented the car, I'd received high octane gas coupons. I had the feeling that those weren't available to the average local motorist. Most Soviet drivers bought the cheap stuff. I drove past the string of cars to the self-serve high octane pump where there was no line.

"40 litres." I shoved my gas coupons through the small glass opening to the cashier. She examined them, then switched on the pump.

With a full tank of gas, I approached a road sign that read "Talinn and the Republic of Estonia." An arrow pointed up into the sky. Another arrow with three roads to choose from pointed toward Petrodavoretz.

For the next hour, I drove in circles, stopping periodically to quiz people on the street, "Where is Petrodvoretz?" One woman didn't know what I was talking about and another sent me down the road to Estonia. A couple of rain-soaked teenage hitchhikers pointed me back toward Leningrad. An over-animated gentleman intricately described his neighborhood, pointed his fingers, made sweeping hand gestures, and bulged out his eyes hoping to enlighten me. I listened cautiously to a fat man who gave me directions while brushing the coat of a monstrous thing that was chained and baring its fangs at me. Then I met a policeman who sensed my uncertain grasp of the Russian language and spoke to me as if I were a moron, pointing out that a small section of the road to Petrodvoretz was closed for repair, and an unmarked detour was in effect.

Sheets of heavy rain started to fall again. I hoped I wouldn't get another flat tire since I no longer had a spare. I'd gotten more flat tires in two weeks on Russian roads than I had in the last three years at home. Peering out the windows, looking for even a hint of the palace, I almost ran over an unmarked, open manhole in the middle of the street.

After awhile, I began to think that every driver knew where to go but me. My American highway sense had been groomed with lighted signs, quivers of roadside arrows, and centerline reflectors. I needed instinct to survive on Russian streets.

Finally, I saw some intriguing ten-foot-high yellow walls, but no sign. I parked my car and asked a man standing in front of a small market, "Where's Petrodvoretz?" He pointed over my shoulder toward the yellow walls. I felt like a dope, standing in front of Mt. Rushmore asking where Lincoln's head was.

I followed a side street, walked through a gate, turned a few corners, and saw a small Cyrillic sign—"Entrance. 30 kopecks."

My mood suddenly brightened as I shelled out the kopecks to buy a ticket and an ice cream bar. I should have used my pocket dictionary to translate the fine print posted at the cashier's window. Tickets varied in price, so I bought the cheapest one and entered the grounds feeling victorious.

The sun broke through the afternoon clouds as I strolled through the palace forests, looking at scores of fountains and golden statues, canals, and gardens.

One fountain resembled a giant colorful mushroom. Forty people could stand under its cap. Hundreds of water jets ringed the sculpture, forming a circular curtain of water. No one knew when the jets would erupt. Sometimes, they went on and off in seconds, and sometimes minutes. People would dart back and forth from the cover of the mushroom, daring a good soaking.

My first leap ended in a dry landing. From under the cap, the jets of water looked like glass columns, an inch or two apart. Several children jumped back and forth, completely soaked, shrieking with laughter every time they got doused. I thought about it too long on the way out and walked around the rest of the day with a wet pant leg.

The winds had subsided and the hydro-foil ferries began to arrive from downtown Leningrad. Most people came to Petro-davoretz by water, landing at the convenient piers where the palace grounds met the Gulf of Finland. I had arrived at the back door.

Peter had an impressive house. The Nazis enjoyed it so much in the forties that they took most of the statues and other antiques back to Germany when they went home. They also trashed the mansion. The Russians had to conquer Berlin to get their treasures back. The government spent millions of rubles to put Peter's house back in order.

I decided to have lunch in an outdoor restaurant on the grounds before touring the palace itself. It was a palace *stolovaya*, a large cafeteria with outdoor seating near the trees and canal. A good lunch cost only a dollar. Four Gypsy women sat at the other end of the table, taking a lunch break from peddling their silver and leather work to palace visitors. I think it was against the law to do that. One of them had accosted me on a remote path in the woods, and practically grabbed me by the lapels to get me to buy something. She didn't seem to remember me.

When I finally decided to see the palace, I discovered that my cheap ticket didn't cover the cost of an inside tour. The ticket booth was closed by then. I tried to sneak in, but a sixty-year-old, iron-willed woman guard wouldn't let me into the inner corridors without a ticket. I'd even managed to get a pair of the required slippers for my shoes to protect the inlaid wood floors. The guard barred my passage with folded arms and a head that swiveled back and forth. I acted disoriented, spoke only in English, and handed her an old ticket stub from the Moscow circus.

"*Nyet.*" She was a veteran.

One of the directors, a bushy-haired younger man with horn-rimmed glasses, asked what country I was from. He smiled, shrugged his shoulders, and turned me away too, but without conviction. As I walked away feeling rejected, he reappeared through a side door out of sight of the older woman. He motioned quickly to me. I followed him through a series of dark passages that led upstairs through the walls of the palace. He nodded to me and opened another door, turning me loose on the second floor of the palace for a self-guided tour. I'd finally reached Petro-davoretz.

✧ ✧ ✧

The color TV buzzed and fluttered for five minutes before it warmed up. I don't know what I expected to find on the Soviet tube at eight o'clock in the evening in the 1100-year-old city of Novgorod, but certainly not Burt Reynolds. Yet, there he was, speaking fluent Russian. That afternoon, I'd seen the marquee of a Leningrad movie theater on Nevsky Prospekt, advertising *The Verdict* with Paul Newman.

I flipped the station. Rows of combines roared impressively across grain fields in the Ukraine. Happy farmers talked about harvesting the crops. I couldn't understand what they said, but I watched for a few minutes before turning it off and heading for the streets. The last sunset colors faded into darkness.

Outside the hotel, a few young men milled around a small plaza. When I crossed the street, one of them broke out of the group and walked quickly toward me, falling in alongside.

"Do you know what time it is?" he asked in Russian. He was tall, with bushy blond hair. His come-on gave away his black market intent.

"*Da*," I pulled my sleeve back, taking the bait and revealing my digital watch. "8:30." I tried to say the time casually so he would think I was Russian and leave me alone. He knew I was a foreigner before I opened my mouth. I'd been easily recognized exiting the Intourist Hotel wearing silver and grey Hi-Tech walking shoes. Novgorod didn't have the cosmopolitan atmosphere of Moscow or Leningrad; it was an old provincial city made dreary by rain clouds and neglect.

The marketeer walked with me down the street, frisking me for my nationality and destination, speaking enough English to say that he wanted to buy my shoes, pants, and watch.

He kept asking how much my clothes cost in America. He liked my shoes, which probably seemed like glass slippers on the streets of Novgorod. I felt the guilty stab of having too much and wanted this sidewalk conversation to end. I'd encountered very few speculators in the five weeks I'd been in Russia. Wearing Soviet shirts and sandals helped me blend into crowds. These streetwise business people moved with the wariness of sidewalk drug dealers in America. Soviet law prohibited speculating in foreign goods and currency, but a lot of people did it anyway.

The tall youth continued walking alongside me until I pointedly told him, "*Ooo menye nyet vyeshee prodavat.*" I have no things to sell.

He nodded, peeled off and jogged back toward his friends. I felt relieved, but my conscience was uneasy. The guy obviously didn't have much. His sneakers were falling apart and his jeans were worn. A lot of young men his age in America already had new cars. He'd left a beat-up, undersized bicycle leaning next to a tree when he came over to me.

I walked downtown and ended up in the city park after dark. A mixed group of old and young people danced around a fountain to a few accordion players squeezing folk tunes out of their instruments. I sat and watched their lightfooted polka steps, before continuing down a dark, tree-lined path toward the river.

A crowd of teenagers gathered outside an open air music arena. High wooden walls surrounded the pavilion and a rock band echoed from inside. The ticket booth was a large windowless box the size of four telephone booths, with a mousehole opening at belt level for transactions. Concertgoers placed their coins in the curved opening and a hand reached out and snatched the money. All you could see were the fingertips.

The person inside the booth mimicked my accent in a high voice, then laughed. That didn't do much for my sense of success at blending into the crowd. I'd only said, "One ticket, please."

A platoon of older men wearing red armbands supervised the dark arena entrance. A few low-wattage light bulbs cast a dim glow on their faces. A muscular guy in a tight-fitting shirt used a stiff shoulder to bump me aside. The faint smell of liquor lingered in his path. I held up my ticket and one of the red armbands nodded me past.

The lights of Novgorod reflected overhead against low evening clouds. Four or five hundred teenagers crowded the pavilion floor, dancing conservatively to a seven-piece, electrified folk-rock group. The lead singer played acoustic guitar and sang through an echo chamber.

After each song, a few people clapped and hooted, but most remained quiet. I was used to noisy American concert crowds. It felt strange to be around several hundred teenagers and have the scuffing of shoes be the loudest sound between songs.

The whole arena was dimly lit, so it was hard to see faces. Red armbands stood stiffly in the shadows watching, while black leather and denim danced to Russian rock.

When the band took a break, several films played across a large screen mounted on a wall. An anti-smoking cartoon showed the devil making everybody smoke, corrupting people's health, and instigating industrial pollution that ruined the environment. Just about every teenager in the place lit up a cigarette while the cartoon played, laughing and blowing smoke at the devil's antics.

In the other film, a teenager from a broken home got punched out by a gang of hooligans. The punky gang leader wore a tight fitting U.S. Marine T-shirt. The crowd loved it.

When the band started playing again, I moved over to a dark wall at the far side of the arena and stood on a bench for a better view of the stage and crowd. I'd been up there about ten seconds when a stern older woman with a red armband showed up out of the shadows and poked me in the arm.

"Nyet!"

She disappeared as soon as both my feet touched the floor. I walked out to the edge of the dance floor and leaned against a pole, half expecting another poke in the ribs.

Instead, one of the dancers in front of me dropkicked some guy in the side of the face with his boot. The fight spread quickly. In a flash, ten people were kicking and punching right in front of me. I stepped back. One group broke off to the side of me. Three guys fighting two. Head punches and Kung Fu feet.

One person went down. Then a stocky, red armband came flying out of the shadows, blitzing like a line backer through the melee with elbows and straight arms flailing. A few of the teenagers got knocked to the ground. The fight stopped. Someone on the floor got a last minute kick in the ribs. The dancing froze, then resumed. The band never stopped.

I stood back against the wall. A tall shadowy figure in a black leather jacket and bushy hair walked up to me in the darkness, nodded his head, doubled up both fists, and made a whirling motion with his hands. I felt a rush of adrenaline. He either wanted to fight, or was motioning about the fight that had just occurred. I didn't know and it was too dark to see his eyes clearly. I watched his hands. He yelled something at me. The music was too loud, I couldn't hear. He stepped toward me. I thought he was going to take a swing, but he bent his head close to my ear.

"*Pomneesh menye? Strachali na gostaneetsoo.*" He shouted over a blaring guitar solo. Remember me? We met near hotel.

The black marketeer. I didn't recognize him in the dark. The lights were behind him, revealing very little of his face.

"*Tantsovat?*" He spun his fists again in the whirling motion, asking me if I wanted to dance with him.

"*Da, tantsovat,*" I yelled back reluctantly. We stepped out to the dance floor. He grinned in an odd way. I couldn't tell if he was assessing me, or if it was the bad lighting. Then I noticed four or five others dancing around us. His friends. They'd been in the fight. The marketeer danced loosely. He leaned over and told one of his friends something. They passed it around and grinned as they watched me.

"You are here alone?" he asked, looking down at my shoes.

"*Da.*" I didn't feel like dancing anymore.

"You leave to Moscow tomorrow?" he asked.

I nodded, watching what his friends were up to. The back of my shoulders felt knotted. My mind raced ahead. It was a long walk back to the hotel, down dark streets.

"Come on, let's go." The tall guy motioned toward the exit. I balked.

"Where to?"

"To my girlfriend, there." He pointed across the arena to the doors. He sensed my discomfort. "I want you to meet my girl-friend, please."

We walked around the crowd. I watched his five friends. They nodded good-bye, still dancing in a cluster. In a few seconds I lost sight of them in the shadows. All the dark figures blended in together. We stopped near the stage.

"Please wait, I have to talk to someone. Don't go away." He disappeared into the crowd again.

I thought about making a quick break for the door, but decided to stick around and see what would happen. The marketeer returned with his girlfriend. She extended her hand toward me with a shy, pleasant smile and said hello. They both took me by the elbow and insisted I dance with them to a fast rock song. I relaxed a little, and began to trust him.

The next song was slow. I walked over to the edge of the stage and watched the guitar player while the couple danced together. But my mind was distracted with a dialogue between my depart-ments of internal security and external affairs.

When the slow dance ended, I told them I was leaving. I lied and said it was only because I had to get up early for a long drive to Moscow. The night had been too weird. I was starting to trust the situation, but still felt jittery, like it could all go wrong in a second. They wished me a good trip. We shook hands and I left.

Outside the arena, I slipped off onto a dark path, taking a different direction back to the hotel. I moved quickly, glancing back over my shoulder. It was difficult to see anything in the soot-black tree shadows.

The accordion music still hummed near the fountain. The folk dancers were still singing traditional songs. Their innocence appealed to me. I walked along a main sidewalk. It was about one o'clock in the morning. The last busses of the night roared along the boulevard. The clouds had thinned. I cut across a parking lot and big grassy field, walking by moonlight along a levy near my hotel.

I wondered if Burt Reynolds had ever heard himself speak fluent Russian.

A cluster of semi trucks jamming the parking lot of a roadside restaurant seemed a good recommendation for lunch. I made a quick U-turn across the highway. Colorful ceramic tiles and varnished trim boards decorated the facade of the country diner.

I took a window table. Several drivers were eating lunch and talking. They probably had a few stories about breakdowns and gas lines. Near Vladimir, I'd seen about forty trucks lined up at the gas pumps.

A waitress walked over and rattled off the day's menu, and waited for me to order. She didn't seem in a hurry as she gazed out the window. My orange Lada was the only car in the parking lot. With its black trimmed interior and gold license plates, it looked like a ladybug in the midst of the big olive-green tractor trailers.

To avoid confusion in ordering, since I hadn't understood much of what she said, I pointed to the next table where a big burly man wearing boots, jeans and a plaid workshirt sat hunched over a plate of food.

"I want that please."

"Tea?"

"*Da.*"

"*Spasiba,*" the woman said quietly, with an amused smile.

The diner didn't look like a place where foreigners stopped. It was a long way from the Metropole Restaurant on Karl Marx Street in Moscow. Actually, it seemed closer to a little trucker's cafe about a hundred miles down the road from my home, called Janet's Cafe, although I doubted this place served cheeseburgers or had Hank Williams on a jukebox.

A three-course meal arrived, balanced over the waitress's arms and fingers. Cabbage soup, cucumber salad and a beef cutlet with bread and potatoes. In the land of tea drinkers, the waitress didn't have a coffee pot handcuffed to her wrist.

During lunch, I watched a group of drivers in the parking lot. A semi was jacked up and a man without a shirt worked feverishly wrestling the duals off the rear axle. His back glistened with perspiration and his hands and arms were smudged with grease. The other drivers assisted him.

I'd seen a lot of roadside repairs along Russian highways, but never a towtruck. If a rig broke down, other drivers stopped to help. I'd also noticed that Soviet motorists were pretty good at breaking a tire off a rim and patching it alongside the road, then remounting it and pumping it full of air. My rented car came with tire irons and a hand pump in the trunk.

I paid my bill and walked out to the car at the same time as the burly driver in the plaid shirt. He asked me where I was from, and then wanted to know who I thought would be the next U.S. president after the November elections. We stood and talked in the parking lot for a few minutes before he climbed up into the cab of his Soviet-built Kamaz tractor trailer rig. A few minutes later, I heard the howl of a starter motor and watched a black cloud of smoke blow from the exhaust stack as the truck lurched back onto the highway.

I walked through the narrow underground passage that wound for nearly a quarter of a mile beneath the Lavra, an historic monastery and museum in the city of Kiev. I was dawdling behind the tour group, curiously observing all the little cave people who lay with varnished complexions, staring at the low ceilings of their carved out sanctuaries. Some of them had been under there for a couple of hundred years, preserved from the elements like mummies.

During their lifetimes, the cadavers had been artists, chroniclers, and monks, some of whom had lived under the earth for twenty years at a time, trying to see the light. I wasn't listening very closely to the guide, a trait I'd developed in school, but the strange little corpses with dark brown leathery skin had funny names like Nikon, Nestor, and Alimpy.

I wanted to take a photograph, but the guide said "*Nelzya*," it's not permitted.

I dropped further back in the passageway until everyone was out of sight, then discreetly raised my camera. The shutter speed was set for a long exposure, without a flash.

Five saints lay shoulder to shoulder, framed perfectly in my wide angle lens. I just needed to focus, and hold my breath.

A burning pain zapped me in the back of the head. I almost dropped the camera.

An angry wasp chased me through the passage, but dissappeared as soon as I rejoined the group. My head throbbed while the tour guide talked. The image of five saints remained undisturbed.

The sound of Kostya's accordian played again and again in my mind, blotting out the muffled roar of jet engines. My seatbelt was fastened tight and I leaned back against the cloth headrest. A virtual ocean of brown and green earth spread beneath the silver wings of the Tupelov airliner as we cruised 30,000 feet over

Russia. My window seemed like a keyhole to a world dotted by tiny islands of towns and cities.

I didn't want to be aboard the Aeroflot passenger jet that day. I wanted to be on the ground, listening to Kostya's songs, walking under the chestnut trees, and drinking tea in the bowl-sized cups that Lena placed around the table. But Soviet travel plans were written in cement. I'd purchased the airline ticket before I left my home in Northern California. Itineraries could not be altered for spontaneous occurrences.

In a city of millions, I'd turned to Kostya and Lena for directions at a crowded bus top. We were looking for the same bus to an outdoor museum of wooden architecture. The historical park was about 30 kilometers outside the city. Lena bought my ticket and invited me to accompany them. I didn't know that Kostya was blind until we were aboard the bus and headed out into the countryside. I spent the day with them walking in the sunlight along paths that wound through forests and hills where more than 200 wooden buildings stood, all resurrected from past centuries.

That evening, sitting around their kitchen table, Kostya's fingers raced over the keys of his silver and black accordion. A wide smile played across the blind musician's face, his head rolling easily, accenting every note, his right foot keeping rhythm. Everyone in the small apartment rode on the edge of his melodic passages, listening to Georgian, Russian, and Gypsy folk songs. Kostya's soulful rendition of Midnight In Moscow left me feeling pensive.

The evening reminded me of parties at home—friends gathered around a big table, simple food, a few bottles of wine, and music. A succession of dinner parties with old friends had spawned the band I had played in for the last nine years. A couple of the guests in Kostya's band had known each other since school days.

"It is best when bands and friends can be together over many years," he said.

Kostya had not been blind all his life. When he was twenty

years old, he studied to be a painter like his father, but his vision ended abruptly one night in an auto accident when he plunged through a windshield. Five operations and fifteen years later, he still lived without eyesight, but retained a great reservoir of humor.

"Zhon! Zhon!" He said, sitting at the table that night, pushing a plate of chicken sandwiches toward me, "More sandwiches? Ha, ha. Tomorrow you will have feathers puck, puck, puck . . ."

"Zhon! Don't drink too much wine." His animation stirred laughter among friends. *"Boool, boool, boool, potom, xryou, xryou, xryou."* Glug, glug, glug, then oink, oink, oink.

"Eta shootka." That's a joke, he'd say, after his comical sound effects and comments.

I kept forgetting that he was blind and gestured with my hands to aid my conversation. Hand signals comprised an integral part of my Russian language ability. I gave Kostya a cassette of our band. He put the tape in his player and turned up the stereo. The other neighbors in the flat didn't seem to mind the pulsing beat of Yankee music.

Lena looked at my photographs of friends, and postcards of Northern California beaches, forests, and a volcano. I felt bad that Kostya couldn't see them, though he was just as interested as everyone else. He sat with a blank canvas before his eyes, listening to Lena intricately describe the details of each picture, his imagination painting the scenes until he too could see the image.

Earlier that evening, Kostya had asked if I wanted to go for a walk and watch the sunset. Lena had gone to the grocery store to get some things for dinner and he wanted to show me a few sights.

The front door to their apartment building opened onto a large asphalt and grass courtyard where a few cars were parked and a dozen children played. Two grandmothers sat on a bench and watched the children. Large chestnut trees lined both sides of the quiet, dead-end street in front of the building.

"Here comes the bus," I said, as we waited on a busy street corner several blocks away.

"That is the wrong bus," Kostya answered. He spoke only Russian. His voice carried in a deep baritone.

"*Kak toy znaesh?*" How do you know?

"It sounds different." The first two busses ran on gasoline. When the hum of an electric bus came, Kostya brushed my elbow, "This is our bus."

We rode the trolley toward the city center, winding through neighborhoods on wide boulevards. The bus ride cost about a nickel. Kostya talked the whole time.

"There is a park over there." He stared straight ahead, but pointed out the other side of the window. "And there is a theater across the street. This is the district where I grew up. I was a small boy once, playing in that park."

The bus stopped more than a dozen times. Kostya kept talking, looking past me from behind his smoke-tinted glasses, occasionally pawing at the air to find my arm. I wondered how he could possibly keep track of where we were.

"Here, we get off," he suddenly interrupted.

"Where are we?" I asked.

"Near the river."

Kostya held my elbow and walked quickly along the sidewalk. I'd known few people who walked as fast as I did.

"I like to walk fast," Kostya said, "This is my exercise, it's good for the health."

Whenever we came to a curb, he always knew whether to step up or down, and which way to turn at each corner, although sometimes he asked the name of the street. While walking back toward their home in the dark, beneath the chestnut trees on his street, I stumbled over a small steel pipe that was fixed across the sidewalk. But Kostya didn't stumble. He held my arm to steady me.

"Sorry," he said, "I should have told you."

"Kostya," I joked, "you are my eyes."

After dinner that night, I took out my melodica, a small wind instrument with a double octave keyboard. Kostya became absorbed in a sound that was new to him. When I handed him the small instrument, he ran his fingertips gently over every surface, then put it to his lips and played as if he'd owned one for years.

One of Kostya's friends, a poet and guitarist in his band, picked up a guitar, and with Kostya, wrote and sang a simple verse about our chance meeting.

Before I left their apartment that night, I gave the melodica to Kostya. His astonishment was translated into enthusiastic speech and gestures. He and Lena both hugged me.

"We want you to have something Russian," Lena said. "For your home in America."

"Our Russian samovar," Kostya pointed toward an ornate electric urn, with a spigot, curved handles. "This is our gift. When you make tea, you will remember us, and this evening."

Lena took the samovar off their shelf and presented it to me. Beneath my appreciative gestures and words, I wondered how I would ever be able to carry the thing halfway around the world without smashing it. The tea-making device was as bulky for traveling as a large crock pot, but delicate. In an instant, Lena boiled water in the samovar to prove that it worked, then disappeared out of the room, and returned with it packed snugly in its factory shipping container with a convenient rope handle lashed around the box.

When I left their home, everyone accompanied me down the street toward the subway station. The guitarist in Kostya's band carried the box. We walked in the warm night air and waited for a bus on the corner. I didn't want to leave this haven of friends, laughter and music. But I was locked into my travel plan — a bus to a subway to a hotel to a taxi to an airplane.

Thirty thousand feet over Russia, I sat and read the words that Kostya and the poet had written down and sung the night before:

> "We all remain in expectation
> In this wonderful September evening
> We'll meet again Zhon, our dearest one
> And we'll sing all together."

Rodina

"I'm absolutely sure if, for instance, (your president) could sit down on the shores of Lake Baikal near a hunter's fire and drink vodka and speak with our fishermen, with workers, and others, he would be a different man, as would many other Americans. And many Russians would be different if they could come to America and sit near a hunter's fire in the Rocky Mountains and speak with Americans." —Yevtushenko—

ndrov threw another log in the fire, then prodded it with a length of steel pipe. Orange sparks swarmed into the early morning darkness. We stared into the flames, listening to the crickets and bull frogs celebrate a full moon over the Kamenka River. Nightingales warbled from a nearby wooded area, first one bird, then another, their songs echoing across the small valley.

Our campfire blazed on a knoll above the river, near the towering white brick walls and eight-story turrets of the former Spasa-Evfimijevsky Monastery. Tule fog hovered around the silent, sixteenth century structure. Androv opened his canvas rucksack, took out a dozen potatoes and buried them carefully in the coals at the edge of the fire.

"These will be good," he said.

"Who wants to swim?" Sasha spoke out across the fire. Androv shook his head no. I didn't want to jump in the river either. It was three o'clock in the morning and we'd been sitting around the fire since midnight.

Sasha, a young construction worker from the city of Ul'yanovsk, jumped up and expanded his chest. "I'm going into the water." He flexed his arms, unfastening the row of tiny plastic buttons on his shirt, then trotted off to the river. A few minutes later I heard a loud splash and a few yelps.

The river was partially hidden by the mist that hugged the lower meadow. I could hear Sasha swimming but couldn't see him except for an occasional luminescent dash of water.

I had walked down to the river hoping to hear the nightingales after having a late dinner in a restaurant. The moonlight made it easy to see the dirt path that wound along the banks of the Kamenka. Androv had appeared out of the fog, walking across a wooden footbridge, and invited me to join him and his friend Sasha around a fire he'd built on the hillside near the monastery.

"How many people are there in the city where you live?" Androv asked, looking curiously over the flame toward me. The two of us had spoken very little that night. He seemed a quiet man, staring into the fire for long periods with a distant look in his eyes. His bearded profile disguised his youth, and by the firelight, I kept seeing him as a small Viking.

"Hmm, about four hundred people."

"Four hundred thousand?" He thought I'd left out a word.

"Nyet, tolka chetearista." Only four hundred.

"Eta mala goradoak." A very small town. Androv lived near Suzdal, he understood the life of small towns.

"In my town," I pointed to the fire, "my friends and I make fires on the beach and sit together until late at night."

"Da, here in the countryside, we do that too." Androv added.

I glanced from the crackling flame to the northern constellations. Nightingale songs echoed around the silhouetted monastery towering above us. The ancient stone walls and bulbous onion domes had sprouted in the wake of Genghis Khan's horseback warriors and the Mongols' two-hundred-year occupation of Russia. The churches and monasteries of Suzdal were now government preserves of art and history.

I tried to tell Androv how glad I was to be sitting by a fire with Russians, along a tributary of the Volga River, surrounded by architecture reflecting a thousand years of culture. Fifty generations bound to Russian soil. Androv listened and nodded his head.

"Our people have a very long history."

I thought about my family—sailing out of the North Sea almost four hundred years ago, bound for the new world. Seventeen generations in America seemed young compared to the Russian millennium.

Androv tossed more wood on the fire. The sudden flare-up of heat felt good against the early morning chill. A cluster of small wooden roofs peeped through the mist on the far bank of the Kamenka. That night I had walked among the newly constructed buildings which were part of a film set. Piles of lumber scraps littered the narrow walkways and fog drifted between dwellings. Androv was the watchman.

A movie was being filmed by Soviet, Italian, and American producers about Peter The Great, the six-foot-eight tzar who forged Russia into a world power at the turn of the seventeenth century.

"Listen," Androv paused. A dog howled a long mournful cry. "Sabaka sings to the moon."

Sasha hustled back to the fire, shivering, wearing only his trousers. Androv looked over at him with an amused grin.

"Androv," Sasha chattered. "How much time before potatoes?"

"Maybe thirty minutes," Androv replied slowly, glancing at the coals.

"*Xarasho*." Sasha took his metal wristwatch from his pocket, flexing his arms and chest. His mannerisms reminded me of a fellow I'd run a jackhammer with one summer working highway construction out in Utah.

After the flames died down, Androv reached into the coals with a stick and flipped a potato onto an open newspaper he'd prepared, then cut into the blackened skin.

"They're ready."

One at a time, Androv uncovered the charred potatoes and pulled them from the fire. He emptied a bag of brown bread and cucumbers onto the newspaper, arranging the food in separate piles.

Sasha threw more wood on the fire and produced a shiny

metal flask from his jacket pocket. *"Vodka xocheesh?"* he offered. We picked away at the food and passed the metal flask around until it was empty.

The sun would be up in a few hours. I stretched out alongside the fire on a patch of grass and leaned back against a small log round. The moon dipped low on the horizon, then vanished from sight.

As the eastern sky lightened, I bid good day to Androv, and walked down the hillside, following the dirt path. The Kamenka still lay partially hidden beneath ground fog. I looked back to the distant hillside and the long white rampart of the monastery. A faint waft of smoke rose pale in the morning light. Androv and Sasha were barely visible, sitting on log rounds near the embers. The nightingales and crickets weren't singing anymore. But the bullfrogs welcomed a new day.

Popular Soviet joke:

A man is sitting on a hill eating lunch in the Ural Mountains. He sees two workers with shovels walk across the fields below him. They both stop, one digs a hole, then they wait five minutes. The second man fills in the hole, tamping it gently. They walk another ten paces and repeat the sequence. This goes on for an hour or so until a dozen neatly lined up holes dot the field. The man on the hill is miffed.

"Shto bweevaeyet?" What is happening? He walks down into the field, approaches the two workers as they pause between diggings and asks, pointing to all the holes, *"Shto vwee de-lighitye?"* What are you doing?

One worker leaning on a shovel replies: We're a three-man tree-planting crew, but the one who plants the tree didn't come to work today.

The old Petropavlovskaya Fortress was a quiet spot to spend an afternoon. Stone walls rose to seal out the city's noise and the dark waters of the Neva River lapped against the buttress of quarried footings that formed a wide promenade along the fort's southern exposure. A few people leaned against the thick rock walls, absorbing the sun's warmth.

I had just emerged from the Cathedral of the Tzars, after an hour with the dead rulers of old Russia. About thirty tzars lay scattered around the floor of the golden spired cathedral, boxed up in sealed marble vaults surrounded by little fences. Gold Cyrillic nameplates identified each miniature tomb.

A bicyclist at the edge of the promenade caught my attention. He was sitting on the stone work, bent over his newspaper. I walked by him three times, hoping to catch his eye, but he never looked up. He wore black cycling pants, a wool jersey, leather cycling shoes, and a small hat with a stunted bill. I knew we would have something in common. Other people strolled along the river's edge, but none of them had racing bikes.

"Excuse me. What kind of bike is that?"

The man looked up. I felt nervous. My Russian sounded odd. He stood up quickly. He was a surprisingly large man, about 6' 4" with energetic movements and an athletic stance. He looked more like a pro football player than an avid cyclist. He didn't quite understand my question. I asked again.

"*Eta Sovietsky velociped?*" A Soviet bicycle?

"*Da. Sovietsky,*" he answered, glancing at his green 10-speed as if it were only a distraction. "You are foreigner. From what country are you?"

I gave him my usual reply, watching his expression. The man's jaw looked as solid as the stone blocks under our feet.

"Oohh, *Americanetz!* Hello, hello! Please sit down here with me." He quickly folded his newspaper into a little mat and placed it on the smooth, cold stone. I wasn't sure what the paper was intended for and started to sit next to it. He took me by the arm, insisting that I sit on the newspaper. "Where in America?"

"California, near San Francisco."

"Have you lost your group?"

"No, I'm traveling alone."

"Alone! In Russia. Ha!" He slapped his knee. "What a surprise. And you are having a good travel? I am glad to meet you. My name is Alexander. Alexander Nikolaiovich." He shook my hand vigorously. "I'm very glad you are here."

I began to relax. It had been hard for me to approach the Russian bicyclist who was so engrossed in his reading.

Alexander spoke in sudden bursts of Russian, often too difficult for me to understand. He pointed across the river toward Leningrad's eighteenth-century skyline, telling me that he worked for the city as an electrical technician, mostly on the subway system. He had also worked at the Hermitage, the tzars' Winter Palace that stretched ornately along the Neva for the length of two football fields. The blue, white, and gold architectural monument now housed one of the world's largest art collections.

He had studied English for six years when he was a young boy in grade school, but he couldn't remember those lessons now. He spoke only in Russian.

"Foreigners in groups from all countries come to the Hermitage," Alexander explained. "Once, I tried to talk to an older Englishwoman in my very bad English for practice."

Alexander stuck his nose up in the air and looked down on me with a snobbish, comical expression, twitching his shoulders back and forth imitating the woman. His size made such petite gestures all the funnier. "She looked annoyed that I tried to talk to her. She walked away."

"Do you want to read newspaper?" He brought us quickly back to the present.

"It is too difficult for me," I replied.

"For practice. I will help you! I have another paper."

Alexander stood up and grabbed a cylinder wrapped in newspaper from one of the water bottle holders bolted to his bike frame. He unrolled it. Vodka. Alexander wagged his finger.

"*Nyet, nyet.* This is not for us. I don't drink or smoke. Bad for health." He pounded on his chest with a fist, then scooted around to face me, sticking out his chin and posing like a statue. "How old do you think I am?"

I studied his face for a moment. He was so physically fit it was almost scary. But the way the question was baited I decided to guess high.

"Thirty-eight."

"Ha, ha!" Alexander Nickolaiovich had a good laugh. "*Nyet.* Forty-seven. It's true! I ride my bike. I don't drink. I don't smoke. This vodka is for my daughter. Today, she is twenty-one years old. Her friends will come to celebrate her birthday."

It was hard to believe Alexander could have a twenty-one-year-old daughter and a teenage son.

We sat along the Neva talking for a couple of hours. He read words aloud from the newspaper and tried to explain what the stories were about. Then he prodded me to read the long, grammatically complicated text and he would correct my pronunciation. After a while, we set the newspaper aside and talked about our lives.

He spoke urgently about our two countries and how we must live as friends, without war.

"*Mir ee druzhba!*" Peace and friendship!

It was happening again. Everywhere, Soviet people insisted that I understand this. Alexander seemed even more emphatic than some of the others. "*Mir ee druzhba*" was starting to sound like a Russian version of "have a good day," except here, people seemed driven by some terrible demon in their past. Most Americans I knew who worked for peace were driven by visions of fire in the future. Soviet cities had already burned in war. Many people had been scarred by the flames.

A Russian policeman in a long grey coat strolled by on his beat.

"In America, police carry guns yes? And people too? *Ploxa.*" Bad, he said. "Here, police don't need guns. It's not as dangerous to live!" Alexander continued. "But in America, I think you have many products. *Xarasho!* That is very good." He gave me the thumbs up sign, nodding agreeably. "That is better than here. But I like Leningrad. It is my city! Good air to breathe. Like the country!"

An older woman in a two-piece swim suit who had been standing in the sun against the fortress wall walked over to us.

"I listen to your conversation." She spoke in Russian. "But I cannot tell what nationality you are. Are you German?"

"No, he is American," Alexander Nikolaiovich said.

"Ohh!" Her face became serious. "We don't want war. Your president speaks with jokes about war." Before I could respond, she held up her right arm. It was covered with scars. Her wrinkled hands clasped and exploded with a sharp sound in her breath. Bombs. She mimicked small pieces of metal entering her body. Shrapnel. The woman put her right foot forward. It was maimed, and twisted to the right.

"From war," she hissed. Her expression was haunted as she spoke of the war. "I was on the front in Leningrad. Three years! I was lucky. I lived. Many didn't. I helped soldiers fight. Many died."

Alexander listened quietly as the older woman narrated her story. Her memories of war plagued her.

"Yes, I remember those days too," Alexander spoke up, surprising me. He seemed too young. "I was five years old when the war started. Eight years old when it ended. Sometimes, all we had to eat was grass, pulled from the dirt. I don't ever want to live that again. And I don't want my children to either."

The woman returned to the fortress wall and sorted through her purse. She came back with something in her hands.

"Here," she offered, "presents for you. Please take these."

She handed me two colorful wallet-sized calenders from Leningrad. I thanked her. Her story had tattooed itself across my heart. I felt fortunate to be there.

I coughed slightly. Alexander jumped up quickly as she retreated back to the wall.

"Don't sit on the ground." He was concerned. "You coughed. You need warmth. Be strong in your health." Alexander hoisted me up by the arm and guided me over to the sun-warmed wall. I felt like I was about six years old and had just coughed in front of my mother. A cool breeze blew along the Neva from the Gulf of Finland. I hoped I wouldn't cough again. Alexander would probably throw me over his back and carry me to the hospital.

"I am interested to know," Alexander said, "What do the older people in America say about Soviet Union?"

"Some are curious about life here. And others are afraid, or think it's bad. They don't like the U.S.S.R."

"Here, I think there are people like that too." Alexander laughed a little, but it was a painful laugh, not humorous.

The woman interrupted her sunbathing again and walked over to us. "Take him to Marsova Polye. He should see that." She held both of my hands between hers.

"O.K." Alexander nodded.

I drove my car across Kirovsky Bridge, following Alexander as he pedaled his bicycle quickly in the flow of traffic. He stopped near a park and we crossed the street to an expansive war memorial garden the size of a large city block. A wide walkway led to the center of the memorial. Alexander grew silent as we approached the small monument.

A wedding group arrived and walked quietly to the memorial to lay flowers and stand in silence before a small eternal flame. Alexander whispered to me, "A tradition. Everyone who marries brings flowers. To never forget those who had to die." In numerous cities, I'd seen wedding parties lay flowers at war memorials.

Almost as an afterthought, Alexander leaned back toward me. "More than 900,000 people died in Leningrad during the war."

I stood for a second, translating the Russian numbers in my mind. Then, they hit me. Hard. Alexander's words welled up out of the earth and through the bottoms of my feet. Just as if every woman, man, and child in San Francisco were gone. Alexander was a little boy eating grass while the bombs fell. One thousand people dying everyday. Every single day for three years. The old woman, a bloodied teenager in the trenches. They'd told me their stories. And I couldn't stop my tears. I just stood there and let the chills pass through me, like I had in the fields of Gettysburg. Over 600,000 Americans killed in the Civil War. Twenty million Soviet deaths in World War II. I'd read the statistics in books and found them impossible to comprehend. But now they touched me.

Alexander nudged my elbow gently and motioned to go. We didn't talk again until we'd crossed the street and entered a park shadowed by trees in fall color. A little girl skipped by wearing a crown of meticulously hand-tied autumn leaves balanced on her head. Her lighthearted motion welcomed me back from the ruminations of war.

I looked over at Alexander. He was right by my elbow, walking his bicycle with his other hand. We strolled the length of the park, teaching each other the English and Russian words for everything we encountered, from drinking fountains and benches, to artists' easels and snack bars. We followed a canal waterway back to my car.

"Oh, oh," Alexander cautioned. "*Militzia*," he laughed quietly, pointing across the street. My car was parked illegally. A policeman with tall black boots stood waiting alongside.

"Problem?"

"*Nyet*," Alexander hushed. "Just wait. He'll get frustrated and leave." He thought it was funny.

We sat down on a park bench and watched the policeman. The officer became agitated, looking at his watch, and all around the lawns for the driver of the car. He put one of his black boots on the bumper, then both feet on the sidewalk. He twitched a black and white traffic wand around in his hand. He wanted to write a ticket.

I told Alexander that in America a truck would come and take the car. It would cost a lot of dollars to get it back.

"No worry," Alexander assured me, "here that doesn't happen." The policeman slowly paced up and down the sidewalk, then finally tired of the wait and continued along his beat. Alexander checked his watch. "I must go. My daughter is expecting her friends in fifteen minutes. I must not be late."

We walked together out onto the street. The policeman was nowhere in sight. Alexander reached out and shook my hand, holding my elbow firmly at the same time. He kept eye contact with me as he said farewell.

"When you go home, tell your friends that here we want to live in peace. For all time." The flame of Marsova Polye flickered in the distance.

"Thirty minutes to the border. Passports prepared please."

I sat up quickly. Thirty minutes to the border! The Soviet border. My pulse beat like a drum.

Nina and her daughter were just waking in their bunks across from me. They greeted the morning lazily. I stepped out of the cabin and paced the corridor while they dressed in privacy.

Byelorussian countryside flashed by. I'd read Western travel accounts and heard stories of grueling luggage searches, rolls of film crudely developed on the spot, and written material confiscated. I'd copied the addresses of people I had met onto a small piece of paper which I folded many times and placed in my shirt pocket.

I hurried to the car bathroom and tore up the original addresses, flushing them a few pieces at a time over at least two miles of track in case a special Soviet patrol searched for discarded information near the border. I checked my watch. Fifteen minutes to the border. I returned to my bunk and leafed through my journals: two months of travel notes.

The sound of footsteps in the corridor brought an image of armed guards. Soviet interrogation. Another knock on the door.

"Ten minutes to the border." The conductor slid the door open. "Passport?" I held up my American passport. He smiled. "Very good." He moved on to the next cabin and left our door open.

I looked over at my cabinmates. Their maroon Soviet passports lay on their laps. Eira's cheek rested against her mother's shoulder.

Eira was seventeen and her mother, Nina, was about sixty. They were traveling to East Berlin to visit relatives. We had left Moscow the previous afternoon. Eira had never been out of the Soviet Union and was fascinated by everything.

The two were a contrast of generations. Both were soft spoken, but Nina had the radiant glow of an older person very proud of her age and self-assured. Her eyes moved slowly and never darted away from contact. She wore no makeup and she had several gold teeth. Eira was definitely a teenager. She laughed a lot and dressed in a modern style. But her eyes were steady, like her mother's.

The train rolled into the Soviet border city of Brest. We bumped to a stop at the customs depot. Several border guards entered each car. Moments later, I heard the boots coming.

A young officer with a pleasant manner and no gun asked for our papers. He took mine first. "*Americanetz,*" he mused out loud. "*Odeen?*" One?

"*Da. Ya pootashestvavayou byez groop.*" Yes, I am traveling without a group.

He complimented me on my Russian language. He stepped out into the corridor with my passport and papers. I could hear his voice. "*Americanetz,*" he told the other guards. A guard with a face resembling Alfred E. Newman poked his head in the door for a look.

An officer of higher rank entered and raised his eyebrows while reading the list of cities and towns I'd visited from my visa. He grinned and asked me if I'd enjoyed my travels. His friendly manner surprised me.

"*Da,*" I answered. "It is very interesting to be an American traveling in your country."

"Were the people good to you?"

"I met a lot of nice people."

The answer pleased him. He asked me a few more questions prompted by his own curiosity, and then asked to see my luggage. I showed him the three pieces—a box, a small soft suitcase and my shoulder bag full of music tapes, journals and rolls of film. I cut the twine and pried into my big box.

The officer turned his attention to Eira and her mother. He asked Nina to step off the train after she showed a thick wad of rubles wrapped in a Soviet newspaper.

When she left the cabin, the officer sifted through my box without disturbing the tight packing job. Samovar, Georgian tea, books, records, wooden Ukrainian boxes. I opened the soft suitcase for his review. He fluffed through my clothes with his index finger.

"*Fsyo normalnaya.*" All was normal. He told me to stay with the train and that he would meet me in one hour to exchange my Soviet rubles for American dollars. Then he left.

I sat dumbfounded. That was it? The Soviet border? What about my other bag? The one with photos, tapes, journals, and camera? What about my mother's maiden name? Who won the world series in 1955? I felt ridiculous for flushing the addresses across Byelorussia.

The train jerked, then slowly rolled forward onto a siding where a platoon of workers descended on the line of rail cars.

The Soviet pit crew worked quickly. In ten minutes, the entire train was hoisted six or eight feet off the ground by a series of enormous hydraulic jacks. All the Soviet wide-gauge wheel carriages were pulled away by hydraulic cables, and replaced by the standard-gauge carriages that all the other European countries used. An ingenious system designed by one of the Russian tzars so invading countries couldn't run their trains on Russian rails.

I walked with Eira through the greasy shop and out a big open door that led to a yard of rusting locomotive components. The sky was gray. It was much cooler now. If there was any interrogation at the border, it came from Eira's curiosity about life in America.

Half an hour later, the train lumbered back to the customs checkpoint. The young officer guided me to a money exchange office and pointed toward a passage with a tiny glass window. A hand reached out the small opening with my passport.

We rolled out of Brest Station with a new set of wheels under the train and Soviet customs behind us. Just west of the city, I saw several Soviet border guards posted at a bridge over a small river. Guards on the other side of the bridge wore Polish military uniforms.

The small river reminded me of the creek on my grandparent's farm in the Sacramento Valley where we used to catch bull frogs and carp. It seemed a rather insignificant boundary. After traversing more than 10,000 kilometers across the largest country in the world, this little creek showed up, signifying the beginning of Polish territory. America's western border was divided by a 5,000-mile-wide ocean.

Polish customs were brief. The clouds had darkened and rain began to fall. Our cabin took on a festive air. We were over the border. To celebrate, Eira's mother pulled out the huge bag of food for a brunch. The cabin became a traveling buffet as she unloaded the satchel.

I'll call it motherly aggression—that woman attacked me with food. The previous evening, she'd shoved food at me until I was stuffed. Now it was starting all over again.

Eira's mother kept saying, "*Koosheet, koosheet.*" Eat, eat.

"I am, I am."

"And you are so skinny. There is much food. Have another of these."

Eira giggled and tried to rescue me. "Mama, mama." She reached out and tried to intercept her mother's outstretched arm that shook grapes and sandwiches at me.

I stepped out into the corridor to have a look out the north side of the train. The conductor asked how things were going with Nina and Eira. He noticed how they'd taken me under their wing for the journey, buying all the tea and supplying all the meals. I blew my cheeks up and gestured a huge stomach. He enjoyed that.

"So you've traveled many places in Soviet Union?" he asked.

"*Xarasho*," he nodded. Since the moment I'd boarded the train in Moscow, the young conductor made me feel like a special guest. He'd just returned from a month-long vacation and said it was difficult to get back to work.

We crossed into East Germany after dark. Eira and her mother stared quietly out the window. They were holding hands and leaning against each other's shoulders.

Nina reached for the food bag again. "One more piece of bread," she urged, "this time, we must eat everything." I shrank at the thought of "everything."

The two were curious about food in California. Was it different? I tried to explain an avocado: pear-shaped, with soft green and yellow meat inside, and a seed the size of a plum; looks like a vegetable, grows on a tree, spreads like butter, and has the skin of an alligator. Next, I tried artichokes. Nina wrinkled her face and said something. I checked my dictionary. She didn't like thistles.

She wondered if there were any mushrooms where I lived. I said there were hundreds. She smiled. "Are forests and mushrooms in California like Russian forests and mushrooms?" she asked.

Down the corridor, a group of Russian tourists had been tipping a few and singing traditional songs, creating a melancholy mood that carried through the corridor into our cabin.

As the train drew near the East Berlin Station, I found the young conductor, thanked him, and gave him a postcard of a giant redwood tree with a personal note written on the back in my best Russian handwriting. After reading the card, he shook my hand for a long time, struggling to say the right words, wanting to make sure I understood how happy he was to meet me. To meet someone from America.

"*Menye tozhe*." Me too.

I went back to the cabin to sit with Eira and Nina. Eira helped me tie up my cardboard box with a better handle. I gave her ten postcards from California and a pocketful of international coins.

We talked until the train bumped to a halt in the East Berlin railway station.

"Please, come to visit us in Siberia, in Novosibirsk." They gave me their best wishes as we picked up our bags.

The conductor waited in the corridor. He carried my heavy box through the narrow passage. We stood for a moment together on the platform and he fumbled for something in his pocket.

"Here, take this," he urged. "My gift to you." He pressed a metallic object into my hand. The brass badge of the Soviet Railways, his official recognition.

I turned and looked back through the deserted railway station. Eira, Nina and the conductor stood together and waved one last farewell to me. It was almost midnight when I stepped into the streets of East Berlin. The spectre of the Berlin Wall crept up on me from the darkness. But I felt optimistic. I had the railway badge in my pocket.

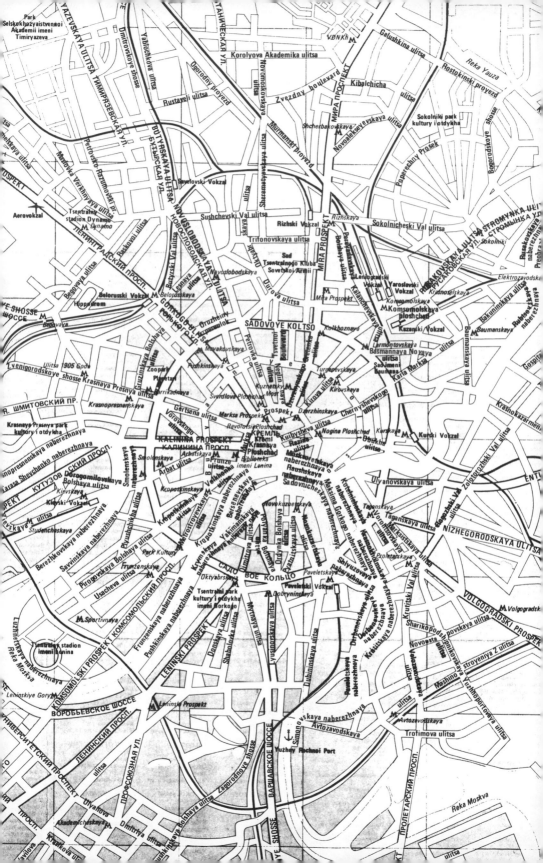

Yuri:
A Soviet Fisherman
in California

Our boat lifted sharply on a big swell, then rolled far to the port side. At the top of the next sea, I focused my binoculars on a Soviet ship that lay just four miles off the northern California coast, near the entrance to Humboldt Bay. The *Ratmonova* drifted in slow motion over moderate swells. Two red smokestacks jutted from the vessel's white superstructure, both stacks emblazoned with a yellow hammer and sickle.

My stomach hollowed as the boat dropped fifteen feet off another wave. The ocean swells were steep and close together on the bar. Jim Walters stood at the wheel of his fifty-foot partyboat, the *Sail Fish*. He'd been hired to transfer Yuri, a young Soviet fisherman, to his ship. He had just spent a week in a local hospital recovering from emergency surgery.

Yuri motioned to my stomach with a spinning motion. "*Chushvavaesh xarasho?*" he asked, wondering if the rolling seas upset my equilibrium. I shook my head and he grinned.

The boat lurched down again. Yuri grabbed the corner of a bench to steady himself, then turned his gaze seaward. Eight days had passed since he'd seen his Soviet crewmates.

The voice of an American observer aboard the *Ratmonova*, boomed in over the radio.

"That's Phillip," Yuri said, pointing toward the radio. Jim reached for the radio mike and answered the *Ratmonova's* call.

The *Ratmonova's* captain would launch one of their lifeboats to rendezvous with the *Sail Fish*.

Jim hung up the radio mike and reached into a box under the instrument console and came up with some printed brochures. "Here's some propaganda," he laughed, handing Yuri some advertisements for his partyboat business.

"Thank you . . . thank you very much." Yuri stammered one of the few English expressions he knew. Our eyes met comfortably. Four days before, we had been total strangers.

The first day I met Yuri, he was asleep in his hospital bed. A ward nurse woke him from his nap. "Yuri, you have a visitor." He scrambled up to a sitting position, wiping his eyes and brushing back his sandy brown hair.

"*Zdrastvweetye.*" Hello.

Yuri looked half awake, but he quickly motioned to a chair. "*Sideetsya pozhalsta.*" He asked me to please sit down. A stack of sports magazines covered the night stand. I noticed vases of fresh flowers at his bedside. We introduced ourselves. His hand felt strong and rough from handling rigging in the salt air.

I told him I'd read in the newspaper about his arrival and wanted to see how he was feeling and to practice my Russian conversation.

Yuri looked surprisingly energetic. He'd had surgery only three days before, but dismissed the appendectomy as, "*choot, choot,*" a little nothing.

I handed Yuri a copy of Ivan Turgenev's play, *A Month in the Country*, printed in Russian. He thanked me, thumbed through it for a moment, then set it aside in favor of our conversation.

We talked for about an hour that first day. He accommodated my vocabulary by speaking more slowly and choosing simpler expressions. Mostly he talked about his family and the sea.

Yuri was twenty-five years old. He'd been at sea for six months, fishing from the coast of North America to the South Pacific Islands. He hadn't seen his family in the past half year, but he and his wife wrote letters and sent messages to each other on the ship's wireless. Yuri and Irina had been married for a couple of years and had a baby daughter. Little Natasha would be one year in just eight days.

Yuri seemed relaxed and in good spirits despite being plucked off this Soviet ship by the United States Coast Guard with five minutes' notice, and dropped into an American hospital for an operation. Nurses hurried in and out on their rounds. Yuri would smile when they tried to talk to him in English. Some of them spoke louder as if he had a hearing problem.

I returned to the hospital the following morning and asked Yuri if he wanted to visit a "redwood factory." He didn't know what the doctor would say. I told him everything had been cleared, the doctor said he needed exercise. Yuri jumped out of bed.

"Please, a moment to prepare."

An hour later, we stood in the Scotia Mill peering through thick glass windows at a monstrous hydraulic debarking machine.

The entire building shook when the big timbers were bounced around by a mechanical monster with claws. It was quite a change from the hospital environment. We walked along on the overhead catwalks stopping periodically to observe various milling stations. Yuri told me the Russian terms for the machines we saw.

He leaned over the railing and watched a multi-ton redwood log roll aboard the band saw's diesel log carriage. It zipped back and forth quickly, peeling off six-inch-thick slabs of lumber.

"*Bweestra!*" So fast, he commented. We stopped to observe a laser-guided edger saw. The re-saw building occupied a floor space equal to a dozen football fields. Yuri was amazed at the size of the mill.

"Near Petropavlovsk we have sawmills." Yuri had to yell above the din of machinery. "But not this big!"

Yuri lived in the largest country in the world where accomplishments were often measured by magnitude. The Soviet Union produced more oil and cement than any country; it boasted the largest merchant fleet, and the biggest airline. Yuri was impressed. The Pacific Lumber Company was the largest redwood mill in the world.

We drove south to Rockefeller Forest where we parked the car and followed a footpath into a grove of giant redwoods. Yuri paused for a moment to look up at the tall trees. Patches of sunlight filtered down onto the fern-covered forest floor. "The quiet—it is beautiful." Yuri looked all around. "I wish Irina could see where I am standing."

Yuri held out a thin gold chain which he wore around his neck. A gold-plated zodiac sign hung from it. Scorpio. "This is Irina's zodiac sign. She wears my zodiac. So we are always with each other."

He tucked the zodiac back into his collar and pulled a pack of Russian cigarettes from his pocket, looking over his shoulder with a joking expression.

"Irina would be angry if she knew I smoked right now. She doesn't like it."

Yuri kept pausing to look up at the great trees. Children's laughter carried up from the nearby Eel River. We stopped.

"Ah . . . *deity*," Yuri said the Russian word for children. We watched about a dozen children and their families picnicking around a swimming hole.

I offered Yuri some blackberries, plums and small tomatoes I had purchased from a roadside produce stand along the highway.

"We must go," I glanced at my watch. "I have to meet other people today. I didn't tell Yuri that I would be late. He would have felt badly. He'd already asked me if I was sure I had enough time to show him around.

"I will always remember these trees," he said, gazing one last time at the tallest trees in the world.

Over the next two days, Yuri toured the far corners of Humboldt County, taking in an outdoor reggae music concert, a museum of Native American basket weavings, a steam powered logging exhibition, and the commercial fishing fleet.

A Russian-speaking doctor from the hospital treated Yuri to the reggae concert, which I attended with some friends. We spent the day together.

At one point during the hot afternoon, I handed Yuri a tuna sandwich and a bottle of mineral water from a cooler while we listened to the rhythmic pulse of a band from Kingston, Jamaica.

Yuri took a few bites of the sandwich and raised one eyebrow trying to figure out what he was eating. "*Shto eta?*" he asked, pointing at his sandwich. I'd mixed in sweet relish so it didn't taste fishy. I didn't know the Russian word for tuna, so I tried to draw a parallel.

"You know about dolphin?" I abstractly linked the two in my mind since they swim together and feed on similar bait. I was about to make the connection, but Yuri heard the word dolphins, and his eyes nearly popped out.

"*Nyet!* Not to eat dolphin!"

"No, no!" I quickly interrupted. "The sandwich isn't dolphin. *Nyet* dolphin." Yuri looked relieved. I fumbled through my pocket dictionary and found the correct word. "*Tunyetz.*"

"Ah, *tunyetz.*" He told about a time when the *Ratmonova* was anchored near Tahiti and a school of dolphins played at the side of the ship with a soccer ball that one of the crew had thrown to them.

Each time we met someone that day, people wished Yuri safe travels, and peace between our countries, the mirror image of my passage through the U.S.S.R. He looked happy and relaxed at the concert. He liked the music, especially the more rock oriented American bands. The huge sound system flooded the valley with music.

"*Xaroshaya shoom.*" I said, confidently. Yuri started laughing.

"*Nyet shoom. Xaroshaya zvuke,*" he corrected, using his hands and ears to indicate something more pleasant. I'd just said it was great noise, instead of sound.

We walked down to the river a few times and waded out into the water to relieve the ninety-degree heat. Yuri's doctor checked his stitches and was amazed at how quickly he was recovering.

Near the end of the day, a friend brought her eleven-month-old baby girl over to meet Yuri. Alyssum's first birthday would be in ten days, within two days of Yuri's daughter's birthday. I told him the little blue-eyed wonder who held his outstretched finger in her tiny grip was the same age as Natasha. For several minutes, Yuri gazed at her. I'm sure he imagined how his daughter had grown while he'd been at sea for the last half year. Yuri cooed little Russian words to Alyssum and pressed his fingers against her chubby arms and cheeks.

"Ya leaubleau deity." I love children.

The next day, we went down to the Humboldt Bay waterfront, where my father's boat was moored. Both my parents were aboard to meet Yuri.

"This boat would probably fit in the hold of your ship," my father joked as he welcomed Yuri aboard. My translation lost the essence of the comment, giving Yuri the idea that my father wanted to drop his boat down the hold of the *Ratmonova*.

We stepped into the pilothouse and Yuri looked around, approving of the electronics.

"Radar, da?" Yuri pointed at the screen. A universal word.

My mother had never met anyone from the Soviet Union before. She'd grown up in American farm country and was interested that Yuri's grandparents raised bees, vegetables, and fruit on their small farm in the Ukraine.

Yuri and my father stood together on the rear deck, near the fish hold, smoking cigarettes, two sailors who loved the sea. When my dad was Yuri's age, he worked as a seaman in the merchant marine. One winter in Vladivostok, friendly Russian sailors sporting vodka bottles took him on a wild sleigh ride down a waterfront street. I waded into that translation but was quickly over my head in sea stories. Yuri and my father wanted to tell each other about ships colliding, towboats, icebergs, and waterfront brawls.

On Yuri's last day ashore, we drove north to Trinidad.

"This is a good highway," Yuri commented, as we buzzed along 101. We passed a purple 1956 Cadillac that had been chopped, channeled, and customized into a bizarre looking pickup truck with chrome "laker pipes" and wide wheels. Yuri eyed it curiously.

"What kind is that car?" he motioned.

"Cadillac." I knew this would be difficult. I tried to explain the American fascination with automobiles. "Some people sculpture their cars."

"Yes? Automobile artists?" Yuri raised his eyebrows, bewildered. It was impossible to explain some things.

"I have a television in my Zhiguli," Yuri stated.

"Say that again."

"There is TV in my car."

"It's dangerous to watch TV and drive, no?" I reached to the dashboard of my car and pretended to change channels and not watch the road.

"No. Not to drive with TV. Only if the car is stopped." Yuri laughed. He had a 4-inch-diagonal TV that plugged into a cigarette lighter. He kept it in the glove compartment and watched it if he had to wait somewhere of if a winter storm hit and he had to pull off the road.

In Trinidad, we walked out onto the headland. A six-foot-wide rocky ledge on the northwest bluffs proved to be a good vantage point. Yuri liked being near the sea again. This was the first time he'd been close to the ocean since coming ashore the previous week.

"Few Russians have ever stood on this rock." I told him that the peg-legged sea captain, Ivan Kuzkoff had been here in the early 1800's when the Russians colonized the north coast of California.

We sat on the ledge and listened. Sea lions barked like a pack of hounds, white water foamed over Trinidad's reef, seagulls uttered shrill cries, and the harbor buoys moaned and clanged.

"This reminds me of home." Yuri was watching the horizon. Somewhere beyond his sight was the *Ratmonova* and his shipmates. And way beyond that was his home and his family.

He described a tradition of his home port. When a ship returned after being at sea, the crew tossed coins into the water around the three large rocks named Three Brothers to repay them for helping them return safely. I told Yuri that ninety kilometers to the north, beyond our sight, were three offshore rocks that protruded from the ocean called the "Three Sisters."

I asked Yuri what his ship did at sea, and what kind of fish they caught. A lot of people in the coastal communities of Northern California thought the Russians were taking salmon. "*Losas, nyet*," no salmon. Yuri said that at home, near Kamchatka, they caught salmon, but off the coast of the U.S. mainland, they only processed hake. None of the Soviet fleet even fished. They were strictly offshore buyers. All the hake were caught by U.S. trawlers and the nets transferred to the Soviets, who cleaned and iced the hake, paying the American fishermen for each net load. One of Yuri's jobs was to handle the rigging as the American nets were winched aboard. U.S. observers were stationed on each Russian ship. I didn't tell Yuri that in waterfront bars, a few chairs had been broken and pool cues swung over the volatile issue of Soviets processing fish in American waters.

"Tomorrow I will go." Yuri spoke with resolve.

"Have you heard yet?" I asked.

"No, but they promised me I would go on Monday."

"Soviet person?"

"Yes, from Seattle. He telephoned me."

"And what if they don't come for you tomorrow?" I asked.

"They will come," he answered, looking out at the vacant horizons.

I looked at my watch. My friend, Beverly, was expecting us for dinner. By the time we reached her house, the August sun was low in the western sky. A couple of puffy clouds navigated the horizon line. Beverly's small house sat on a cliff about two hundred feet above the ocean. We could see thirty miles down the coast almost to Cape Mendocino. It was like being aboard a ship. The grassy cliff extended out about forty feet, then dropped to the ocean. Yuri stood staring to the south and then to the north. "To live so close to sea is very good."

Irina's parents had built a small *dacha* on the Kamchatka

Coast, just outside Petropavlovsk. Their windows looked onto the Pacific Ocean from the east. Our sunset would be their sunrise.

The three of us sat down at a table next to a large open window. The sounds and smells of the seashore drifted in. Cardboard boxes cluttered the house. Beverly apologized to Yuri for the mess and had me explain that she was in the midst of moving in.

Yuri was curious about the cost of housing in the U.S. He folded his hands and looked as if he were swallowing a horse pill as he contemplated the numbers.

"We pay $12.50 a month for our apartment," he said. That wasn't much considering that he made $800 a month, four times the average Soviet wage. But he had to be away from home for months at a time.

Beverly placed a small, nicely wrapped box on the table in front of him. He looked startled. "For Natasha," she said. "It's a birthday present."

"Oh, *spasiba*." His calloused fingers gently unwrapped the package. He lifted a tiny pair of fur-lined snow boots from the colorful box. Yuri seemed on the verge of tears.

"I want to work here."

He wants to work here? In America? In California? Oh, great.

"I don't understand."

"I want to work here. To help move things in the new home." He motioned toward the pile of boxes in the room. "Please. I love to work." Panic retreated in the face of comic relief. Yuri wanted to help Beverly move things. He was already up on his feet, pointing to the furniture, boxes, firewood, anything. "I want to help you. Yes?"

I couldn't help laughing. "No, please, Yuri. You are in the hospital. Remember? Please don't work, O.K?"

Our small gifts and hospitality had tipped the scales and unleashed the Russian passion for reciprocation. One more gift, and he might paint the house.

Toward sunset, we lit a fire in a rock-lined fire pit. Beverly brought out a large cast iron skillet of potatoes, onions, and herbs and placed it over one corner of the fire on a grill. Over the flames, we could see the waves as the smoke drifted to the south.

Yuri looked interested in the food. He hadn't enjoyed some of the hospital meals. At one lunch, he'd sniffed suspiciously at a leaf of lettuce, taken a bite, and wrinkled his face. "Bad cabbage." He missed his Russian bread and thought the spongy hospital bread tasted like cotton.

"It's good to sit in front of a fire again," Yuri said, gazing into the coals. "I can watch fire all night. It's better than TV."

Yuri talked about the Srednaya Mountains where he and Irina hiked. They camped in the forest with a tent, and cooked over the open flame. In the winter, they skied cross country into the mountains and soaked in natural hot pools near a volcano.

"Everything is simple then," Yuri said. "I've got a car and stereo, very interesting things, but people lived for many years without them. We can't live without fire."

We sat by the fire as the night sky unleashed diamonds. It didn't matter that Yuri was from Russia, or that Beverly and I were Americans. Sitting around a fire eating potatoes, people could just be themselves.

At 11:30 the next morning I called the hospital and the ward nurse told me that Yuri's ship had arrived off the Humboldt coast. But he had no idea what was going on. I drove to the hospital to translate the news.

When I walked into Yuri's room, he was reading. I told him that in thirty minutes he would be leaving the hospital to meet his ship.

"Yes?" He was enthusiastic.

He quickly got up, showered, and dressed. A nurse brought a lunch tray for him. He poked through it, eating only half a sandwich and drinking a cup of tea. He seemed anxious. He made brief phone calls to thank two local Russian-speaking people who had also befriended him during his stay in Humboldt County.

At noon, the stevedore agent strode in. I offered to accompany Yuri out to sea as a friend and interpreter. The agent agreed and handed Yuri his passport and some other documents. He signed a few more papers at the ward desk, and said his good-byes. We hurried down to the car and drove out to the south bay community of King Salmon. The *Sail Fish* was waiting.

Yuri and I watched his ship out the windows. The name, *Ratmonova,* stood out clearly in large, white Cyrillic letters against the black steel hull. Smoke billowed from the double stacks. White water boiled at its stern. The three-hundred-foot ship swung around to face a northeasterly direction. It hardly rolled.

Jim cut back the *Sail Fish*'s throttle as we moved in on the leeward side of the giant fishing vessel. I could make out faces of crewmen that lined the rails. Four men scampered up a narrow ladder into the *Ratmonova's* starboard lifeboat. Almost immediately, winches lowered the smaller vessel down the side of the ship into the water. The enclosed lifeboat bore an odd resemblance to a red fiberglass septic tank.

Yuri and I stepped down into the galley.

"Write me if you can," I said. "And good luck. You are a dear friend to me." My simplistic Russian always left me short of what I wanted to say. I handed him a cassette tape of our band's music. The title seemed tailored for the moment, *Sail Away.* Yuri shook his head and thanked me.

"You are friend too. I will always remember you." We shook hands one last time. "*Shastleevway.*"

Yuri turned quickly and stepped out onto the rear deck. The *Ratmonova's* lifeboat came in alongside the *Sail Fish.* Both boats rolled in the seas, lifting ten to twelve feet then dropping. A salty, stubble-faced Soviet seaman smoking a cigar and wearing an orange hard hat, maneuvered the lifeboat close.

"*Kak delo?*" One of the sailors yelled over the clatter of diesels and splashing waves to Yuri. How are things going?

"*Ochen xarasho,*" he yelled back. Really good.

Yuri turned for a last glance good-bye, then stepped up onto the rail of the *Sail Fish.* Both boats rose on the top of another sea. The global separation of our two countries diminished to a four-foot space of turbulent water. Yuri jumped the void. His mates caught him. I threw his bag through the forward hatch to a third seaman who gave me thumbs up. The Soviet lifeboat veered away. And that was it. Yuri had left America and was back aboard his ship. He waved from the open hatch a couple of times before they reached the *Ratmonova.*

Yuri and his shipmates made it safely aboard. I watched them climb down the narrow ladder to the ship's main deck and disappear through an open doorway. Once again the radio blared.

"*Sail Fish.* This is *Ratmonova.* On behalf of the Captain and the crew, we would like to thank you and the agent for all that has been done and the great care you have taken to assist our crewman."

Jim handed me the mike. "Go ahead, they want to talk to the agent."

I wasn't exactly the agent, but I took the gray plastic mike, and pushed the broadcast button.

"Thank you, crew of the *Ratmonovna.* I wish you safe travels at sea." I finished the broadcast in Russian thinking that it might surprise the captain to hear his native language over the American marine radio. "We were all happy to meet Yuri. Now, his health is good. I hope that in the future, the Soviet Union and America will live together in friendship and peace. Thank you. May good fortune be with you. *Sail Fish,* out."

Jim turned east toward the Humboldt Bar and opened up the throttle on both diesels. Black smoke rose from the *Ratmonova's* double stacks. The Soviet ship turned northwest, powering over the tops of the swells.

"This is the *Ratmonova.* The captain has a message for you."

"Viva, America! *Ratmonova,* out."

All photographs in *Soviet Passage*, including those by Tom Pagano and Phil Greenberg, are excerpted from "Behind the Curtain," a mixed-media slide presentation produced by Jon Humboldt Gates. Soft-fade color slide projection choreographed to Russian rock music evokes a journey through Soviet imagery and sound. For information and booking, write:

Behind the Curtain
P.O. Box 911
Trinidad, CA 95570

Photos by the author except where otherwise indicated.

page 53	The Soviet passenger ship, *Khabarovsk*.
page 54	Kiosk selling *Pravda* and Pepsi.
page 55	A farmer selling pears in the produce market. *Phil Greenberg*
	Admiring a baby in Kiev. *Tom Pagano*
page 56	Relaxing under the trees of the Trinity-Sergius Monastery in the town of Zagorsk.
page 58	Galina and her *balalaika*.
	On the outskirts of Listvanka, Siberia.
page 59	Anton in his yard.
	Window detail from private residence in Suzdal.
page 60	Jake from Siberia. Courtesy of Erik.
	An American married to a woman from Moscow invited me to a party at her parents' home.

About the Author

Jon Humboldt Gates was born in Humboldt County, California in 1950. He has worked as a professional musician, deckhand, construction worker, ski bum, market researcher, and lecturer. His first two books, *Falk's Claim* and *Night Crossings* are accounts of regional folk stories. Gates has traveled over 15,000 miles in the Soviet Union in 1984 and 1987, and is currently at work on his American accent.